Looking at an Angle

BRITANNICA
Mathematics
...xt

Geometry and Measurement

TEACHER'S GUIDE

HOLT, RINEHART AND WINSTON

Mathematics in Context is a comprehensive curriculum for the middle grades. It was developed in 1991 through 1997 in collaboration with the Wisconsin Center for Education Research, School of Education, University of Wisconsin-Madison and the Freudenthal Institute at the University of Utrecht, The Netherlands, with the support of the National Science Foundation Grant No. 9054928.

The revision of the curriculum was carried out in 2003 through 2005, with the support of the National Science Foundation Grant No. ESI 0137414.

National Science Foundation

Opinions expressed are those of the authors
and not necessarily those of the Foundation.

Feijs, E., deLange, J., van Reeuwijk, M., Spence, M., S., Brendefur, J., and Pligge, M., A. (2006). *Looking at an angle.* In Wisconsin Center for Education Research & Freudenthal Institute (Eds.), Mathematics in Context. Chicago: Encyclopædia Britannica, Inc.

The Teachers Guide for this unit was prepared by David C. Webb, Sarah Ailts, Jill Vettrus, Els Feijs, Jan de Lange, and Mieke Abels.

ISBN 0-03-039832-0

3 4 5 6 073 09 08 07

The *Mathematics in Context* Development Team

Development 1991–1997

The initial version of *Looking at an Angle* was developed by Els Feijs, Jan deLange, and Martin van Reeuwijk. It was adapted for use in American schools by Mary S. Spence, and Jonathan Brendefur.

Wisconsin Center for Education

Research Staff

Thomas A. Romberg
Director

Gail Burrill
Coordinator

Joan Daniels Pedro
Assistant to the Director

Margaret R. Meyer
Coordinator

Freudenthal Institute Staff

Jan de Lange
Director

Els Feijs
Coordinator

Martin van Reeuwijk
Coordinator

Project Staff

Jonathan Brendefur	Sherian Foster	Mieke Abels	Jansie Niehaus
Laura Brinker	James A, Middleton	Nina Boswinkel	Nanda Querelle
James Browne	Jasmina Milinkovic	Frans van Galen	Anton Roodhardt
Jack Burrill	Margaret A. Pligge	Koeno Gravemeijer	Leen Streefland
Rose Byrd	Mary C. Shafer	Marja van den Heuvel-Panhuizen	
Peter Christiansen	Julia A. Shew	Jan Auke de Jong	Adri Treffers
Barbara Clarke	Aaron N. Simon	Vincent Jonker	Monica Wijers
Doug Clarke	Marvin Smith	Ronald Keijzer	Astrid de Wild
Beth R. Cole	Stephanie Z. Smith	Martin Kindt	
Fae Dremock	Mary S. Spence		
Mary Ann Fix			

Revision 2003–2005

The revised version of *Looking at an Angle* was developed by Jan deLange and Els Feijs. It was adapted for use in American schools by Margaret A. Pligge.

Wisconsin Center for Education

Research Staff

Thomas A. Romberg
Director

Gail Burrill
Editorial Coordinator

David C. Webb
Coordinator

Margaret A. Pligge
Editorial Coordinator

Freudenthal Institute Staff

Jan de Lange
Director

Mieke Abels
Content Coordinator

Truus Dekker
Coordinator

Monica Wijers
Content Coordinator

Project Staff

Sarah Ailts	Margaret R. Meyer	Arthur Bakker	Nathalie Kuijpers
Beth R. Cole	Anne Park	Peter Boon	Huub Nilwik
Erin Hazlett	Bryna Rappaport	Els Feijs	Sonia Palha
Teri Hedges	Kathleen A. Steele	Dédé de Haan	Nanda Querelle
Karen Hoiberg	Ana C. Stephens	Martin Kindt	Martin van Reeuwijk
Carrie Johnson	Candace Ulmer		
Jean Krusi	Jill Vettrus		
Elaine McGrath			

Contents

Dear Teacher,

Welcome! *Mathematics in Context* is designed to reflect the National Council of Teachers of Mathematics *Principles and Standards for School Mathematics* and the results of decades of classroom-based education research. *Mathematics in Context* was designed according to the principles of Realistic Mathematics Education, a Dutch approach to mathematics teaching and learning. In this approach, mathematical content is grounded in a variety of realistic contexts in order to promote student engagement and understanding of mathematics. The term *realistic* is meant to convey that the contexts and mathematics can be made "real in your mind." Rather than relying on you to explain and demonstrate generalized definitions, rules, or algorithms, students investigate questions directly related to a particular context and develop mathematical understanding and meaning from that context.

The curriculum encompasses nine units per grade level. This unit is designed to be the last unit in the Geometry and Measurement strand, but it also lends itself to independent use—to introduce students to calculating the steepness, or the ratio of height to distance, of a right triangle, and to finding the relationship between the angles and the lengths of the sides of a right triangle.

In addition to the Teacher's Guide and Student Books, *Mathematics in Context* offers the following components that will inform and support your teaching:

- *Teacher Implementation Guide,* **which provides an overview of the complete system and resources for program implementation;**
- *Number Tools* and *Algebra Tools,* **which are blackline master resources that serve as intervention sheets or practice pages to support the development of basic skills and extend student understanding of concepts developed in Number and Algebra units; and**
- *Mathematics in Context Online,* **which is a rich, balanced resource for teachers, students, and parents looking for additional information, activities, tools, and support to further students' mathematical understanding and achievements.**

Thank you for choosing *Mathematics in Context.* We wish you success and inspiration!

Sincerely,

The Mathematics in Context Development Team

Looking at an Angle and the NCTM Principles and Standards for School Mathematics for Grades 6–8

The process standards of Problem Solving, Reasoning and Proof, Communication, Connections, and Representation are addressed across all *Mathematics in Context* units.

In addition, this unit specifically addresses the following PSSM content standards and expectations:

Geometry

In grades 6–8, all students should:

- create and critique inductive and deductive arguments concerning geometric ideas and relationships, such as congruence, similarity, and the Pythagorean relationship;
- draw geometric objects with specified properties, such as side lengths or angle measures;
- use two-dimensional representations of three-dimensional objects to visualize and solve problems;
- use visual tools to represent and solve problems;
- use geometric models to represent and explain numerical and algebraic relationships; and
- recognize and apply geometric ideas and relationships in areas outside the mathematics classroom, such as art, science, and everyday life.

In grades 9–12, all students should:

- use trigonometric relationships to determine lengths and angle measures and
- use geometric ideas to solve problems in, and gain insights into, other disciplines and other areas of interest such as art and architecture.

Measurement

In grades 6–8, all students should:

- understand both metric and customary systems of measurement;
- understand relationships among units and convert from one unit to another within the same system;
- select and apply techniques and tools to accurately find length and angle measures to appropriate levels of precision; and
- solve problems involving scale factors, using ratio and proportion.

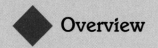

Math in the Unit

Prior Knowledge

This unit assumes that students have an under-standing of:

- metric measurements;
- ratio tables;
- how to use a compass card or protractor to measure angles;
- relationships between ratios, decimals, and fractions;
- equivalent ratios, decimals, and fractions;
- how to compute areas;
- information that is embedded in two-dimensional representations of three-dimensional situations;
- properties of triangles (especially right triangles);
- the construction of triangles;
- scale as used in drawings and maps; and
- line graphs.

In *Looking at an Angle,* the last unit of the Geometry strand, different concepts are formal-ized. Investigating a model of the Grand Canyon, students identify lines of sight, or vision lines. They figure out, for example, from which places on the rim of the Grand Canyon the river can be seen and why it cannot be seen from other vantage points.

Then they use vision lines to determine the blind spot of the captain of different ships in which a swimmer or small boat will not be seen. They dis-cover the relationship between the length of the blind spot and the measure of the angle between the vision line and the water surface. Students also use graph paper and toy boats to investigate the size and shape of the blind spot of different boats.

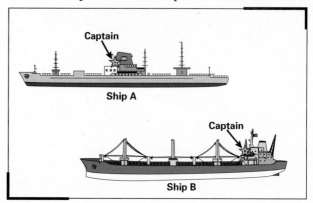

Students explore the movement of the sun and the effect on the direction and length of shadows and the angle of the sun's rays. They describe differ-ences between shadows caused by the sun and shadows caused by a nearby light source. Students learn that shadows are similar to blind spots or blind areas.

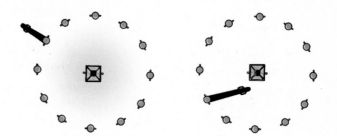

The steepness of a vision line, of the sun's rays, of a ladder, and of the flight path of a hang glider can all be modeled by a right triangle. This leads to formalization of the use of the Pythagorean theorem and its reverse. Students also learn about two other ratios between the sides of a right triangle, the sine and the cosine, which are then used in solving problems.

$$\sin \alpha = \frac{\textit{side opposite } \alpha}{\textit{hypotenuse}} = \frac{BC}{AC}$$

$$\cos \alpha = \frac{\textit{side adjacent to } \alpha}{\textit{hypotenuse}} = \frac{AB}{AC}$$

The context of a ladder leaning against a wall is again similar to that of a vision line or a light ray. It is used to formalize the concept of steepness, which can be determined by either the angle between the ladder and the ground or the ratio of the height to the distance. Students learn that situations similar to that of the ladder can be represented by right triangles.

When students have finished this unit, they:

- understand and use the concept of vision lines;
  - Students model situations and solve problems involving vision lines, blind spots, and blind areas.
  - They understand the relationship between vision lines and blind spots, and sun's rays and shadows.
  - They understand the difference between shadows caused by the sun and shadows caused by a nearby light source.

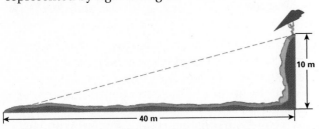

The path of a hang glider is used to introduce the tangent ratio and to formalize students' understanding of it. Students compare the performance of different hang gliders by considering their glide ratio: the ratio between the height from which a hang glider takes off and the distance it covers. They learn how glide ratios can also be expressed as fractions or decimals. Students' understanding of the glide ratio is formalized as the tangent ratio, which they use to solve problems.

- understand and use the concept of tangent, sine and cosine; and
  - Students use previous knowledge of ratio, proportion, angle, and angle measure.
  - They develop informal understanding of tangent ratio by studying blind spots, shadows, steepness, and glide ratios.
  - They develop formal notation and solve problems involving tangent, sine and cosine.
  - Students use a calculator to find the tangent of an angle and the reverse operation.
  - Students explore the relationship between slope and glide ratio (tan α).

- know and use the Pythagorean theorem and its reverse.

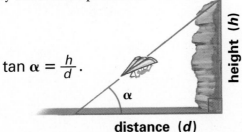

$$\tan \alpha = \frac{h}{d}.$$

distance (d)

Geometry and Measurement Strand: An Overview

In the MiC units, measurement concepts and skills are not treated as a separate strand. Many measurement topics are closely related to what students learn in geometry. The Geometry and Measurement units contain topics such as similarity, congruency, perimeter, area, and volume. The identification of and application with a variety of shapes, both two-dimensional and three dimensional, is also addressed.

The developmental principles behind geometry in *Mathematics in Context* are drawn from Hans Freudenthal's idea of "grasping space." Throughout the strand, ideas of geometry and measurement are explored. Geometry includes movement and space—not just the study of shapes. The major goals for this strand are to develop students' ability to describe what is seen from different perspectives and to use principles of orientation and navigation to find their way from one place to another.

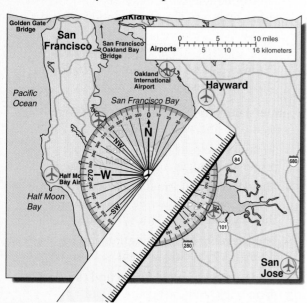

The emphasis on spatial sense is related to how most people actually use geometry. The development of students' spatial sense allows them to solve problems in the real world, such as identifying a car's blind spots, figuring out how much material to buy for a project, deciding whether a roof or ramp is too steep, and finding the height or length of something that cannot be measured directly, such as a tree or a building.

Mathematical content

In *Mathematics in Context*, geometry is firmly anchored in the physical world. The problem contexts involve space and action, and students represent these physical relationships mathematically.

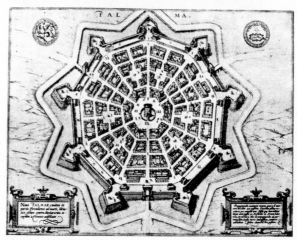

Throughout the curriculum, students discover relationships between shapes and develop the ability to explain and use geometry in the real world. By the end of the curriculum, students work more formally with such geometric concepts as parallelism, congruence, and similarity, and use traditional methods of notation as well.

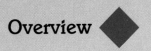

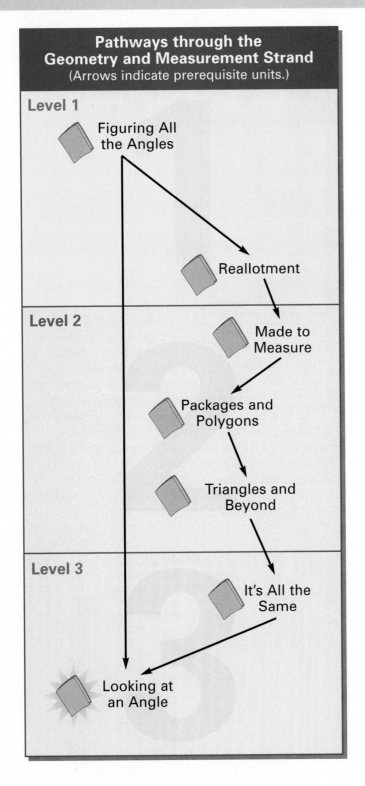

Pathways through the Geometry and Measurement Strand
(Arrows indicate prerequisite units.)

Level 1

Figuring All the Angles

Reallotment

Level 2

Made to Measure

Packages and Polygons

Triangles and Beyond

Level 3

It's All the Same

Looking at an Angle

Organization of the Geometry and Measurement Strand

Visualization and representation is a pervasive theme in the Geometry strand and is developed in all of the Geometry and Measurement strand units. The units are organized into two substrands: Orientation and Navigation, and Shape and Construction. The development of measurement skills and concepts overlaps these two substrands and is also integrated throughout other *Mathematics in Context* units in Number, Algebra, and Data Analysis.

Orientation and Navigation

The Orientation and Navigation substrand is introduced in *Figuring All the Angles*, in which students are introduced to the cardinal, or compass, directions and deal with the problems that arise when people in different positions describe a location with directions. Students use maps and compass headings to identify the positions of airplanes. They look at angles as turns, or changes in direction, as well as the track made by a sled in the snow. They discern different types of angles and learn formal notations and terms: vertex, $\angle A$, and so on. The rule for the sum of the angles in a triangle is informally introduced. To find angle measurements students use instruments such as a protractor and compass card.

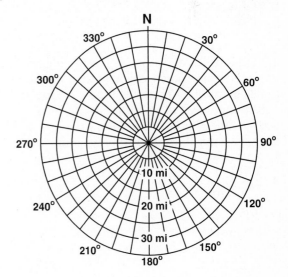

In *Looking at an Angle,* the last unit in the Geometry strand, the tangent ratio is informally introduced. The steepness of a vision line, the sun's rays, a ladder, and the flight path of a hang glider can all be modeled by a right triangle. Considering the glide ratio of hang gliders leads to formalization of the tangent ratio. Two other ratios between the sides of a right triangle are introduced, the sine and the cosine. This leads to formalization of the use of the Pythagorean theorem and its converse.

Shape and Construction

Reallotment is the first unit in the Shape and Construction substrand. Students measure and calculate the perimeters and areas of quadrilaterals, circles, triangles, and irregular polygons. Students learn and use relations between units of measurement within the Customary System and the Metric System.

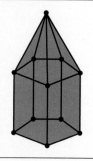

Does Euler's formula work for a five-sided tower? Explain your answer

Solids are introduced in *Packages and Polygons.* Students compare polyhedra with their respective nets, use bar models to understand the concept of rigidity, and use Euler's formula to formally investigate the relationships among the numbers of faces, vertices, and edges of polyhedra.

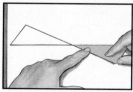
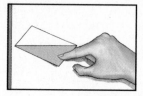

In *Triangles and Beyond,* students develop a more formal understanding of the properties of triangles, which they use to construct triangles. The concepts of parallel lines, congruence, and transformation are introduced, and students investigate the properties of parallel lines and parallelograms. A preformal introduction to the Pythagorean theorem is presented.

After studying this unit, students should be able to recognize and classify triangles and quadrilaterals. In the unit *It's All the Same,* students develop an understanding of congruency, similarity, and the properties of similar triangles and then use these ideas to solve problems. Their work with similarity and parallelism leads them to make generalizations about the angles formed when a transversal intersects parallel lines, and the Pythagorean theorem is formalized.

If a triangle has a right angle, then the square on the longest side has the same area as the other two combined.

Measurement

The concept of a measurement system, standardized units, and their application overlaps the sub-strands of Orientation and Navigation, and Shape and Construction. Furthermore, the development and application of measurement skills is integrated throughout units in the Number, Algebra, and Data Analysis strands, through topics such as use of ratio and proportion, finding and applying scale factors, and solving problems involving rates (for instance, distance-velocity-time relationships).

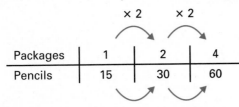

	×2	×2
Packages	1	2	4
Pencils	15	30	60

In *Mathematics in Context*, the Metric System is used not only as a measurement system, but also as a model to promote understanding of decimal numbers.

The unit *Made to Measure* is a thematic measurement unit where students work with standard and non-standard units to understand the systems and processes of measurement. They begin by studying historic units of measure such as foot, pace, and fathom (the length of outstretched arms). Students use their own measurements in activities about length, area, volume, and angle and then examine why standardized units are necessary for each.

The relationships between measurement units are embedded in the number unit, *Models You Can Count On*, where students explore conversions between measures of length within the Metric System. The measurement of area in both Metric and Customary Systems is explicitly addressed in the unit *Reallotment*. Students also learn some simple relationships between metric and customary measurement units, such as 1 kilogram is about 2.2 pounds, and other general conversion rules to support estimations across different measurement systems. In *Reallotment, Made to Measure*, and *Packages and Polygons*, the concepts of volume and surface area are developed. Strategies that were applied to find area measurements in *Reallotment* are used to derive formulas for finding the volume of a cylinder, pyramid, and cone.

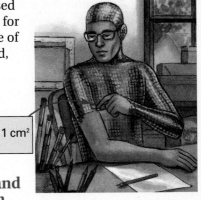

Visualization and Representation

Visualization and representation is a component of every geometry unit. In *Mathematics in Context*, this theme refers to exploring figures from different perspectives and then communicating about their appearance or characteristics.

In *Reallotment*, students use visualizations and representations to find the areas of geometric figures. They decide how to reshape geometric figures and group smaller units into larger, easy-to-count units. They also visualize and represent the results for changing the dimensions of a solid. In the unit *It's All the Same*, students visualize triangles to solve problems.

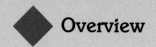

Student Assessment in Mathematics in Context

As recommended by the NCTM *Principles and Standards for School Mathematics* and research on student learning, classroom assessment should be based on evidence drawn from several sources. An assessment plan for a *Mathematics in Context* unit may draw from the following overlapping sources:

- **observation**—As students work individually or in groups, watch for evidence of their understanding of the mathematics.
- **interactive responses**—Listen closely to how students respond to your questions and to the responses of other students.
- **products**—Look for clarity and quality of thought in students' solutions to problems completed in class, homework, extensions, projects, quizzes, and tests.

Assessment Pyramid

When designing a comprehensive assessment program, the assessment tasks used should be distributed across the following three dimensions: mathematics content, levels of reasoning, and difficulty level. The Assessment Pyramid, based on Jan de Lange's theory of assessment, is a model used to suggest how items should be distributed across these three dimensions. Over time, assessment questions should "fill" the pyramid.

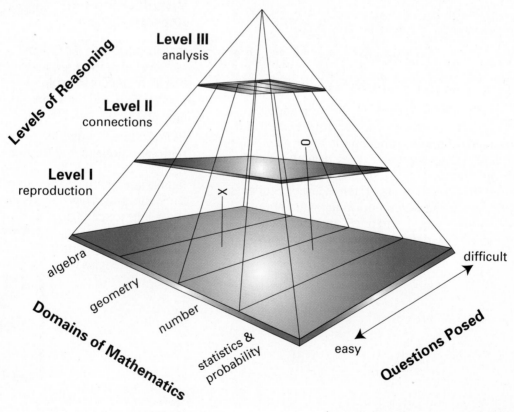

Levels of Reasoning

Level I questions typically address:

- recall of facts and definitions and
- use of technical skills, tools, and standard algorithms.

As shown in the pyramid, Level I questions are not necessarily easy. For example, Level I questions may involve complicated computation problems. In general, Level I questions assess basic knowledge and procedures that may have been emphasized during instruction. The format for this type of question is usually short answer, fill-in, or multiple choice. On a quiz or test, Level I questions closely resemble questions that are regularly found in a given unit substituted with different numbers and/or contexts.

Level II questions require students to:

- integrate information;
- decide which mathematical models or tools to use for a given situation; and
- solve unfamiliar problems in a context, based on the mathematical content of the unit.

Level II questions are typically written to elicit short or extended responses. Students choose their own strategies, use a variety of mathematical models, and explain how they solved a problem.

Level III questions require students to:

- make their own assumptions to solve open-ended problems;
- analyze, interpret, synthesize, reflect; and
- develop one's own strategies or mathematical models.

Level III questions are always open-ended problems. Often, more than one answer is possible and there is a wide variation in reasoning and explanations. There are limitations to the type of Level III problems that students can be reasonably expected to respond to on time-restricted tests.

The instructional decisions a teacher makes as he or she progresses through a unit may influence the level of reasoning required to solve problems. If a method of problem solving required to solve a Level III problem is repeatedly emphasized during instruction, the level of reasoning required to solve a Level II or III problem may be reduced to recall knowledge, or Level I reasoning. A student who does not master a specific algorithm during a unit but solves a problem correctly using his or her own invented strategy may demonstrate higher-level reasoning than a student who memorizes and applies an algorithm.

The "volume" represented by each level of the Assessment Pyramid serves as a guideline for the distribution of problems and use of score points over the three reasoning levels.

These assessment design principles are used throughout *Mathematics in Context*. The Goals and Assessment charts that highlight ongoing assessment opportunities—on pages xvi and xvii of each Teacher's Guide—are organized according to levels of reasoning.

In the Lesson Notes section of the Teacher's Guide, ongoing assessment opportunities are also shown in the Assessment Pyramid icon located at the bottom of the Notes column.

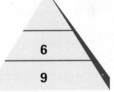

Understand the ratio between an object and its shadow caused by the sun for different times of the year.

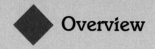

Goals and Assessment

In the *Mathematics in Context* curriculum, unit goals, organized according
to levels of reasoning described in the Assessment Pyramid on page xiv,
relate to the strand goals and the NCTM *Principles and Standards for
School Mathematics*. The *Mathematics in Context* curriculum is designed
to help students demonstrate their understanding of mathematics in
 each of the categories listed below. Ongoing
assessment opportunities are also indicated on
their respective pages throughout the Teacher's
Guide by an Assessment Pyramid icon.

It is important to note that the attainment of
goals in one category is not a prerequisite to
attaining those in another category. In fact,
students should progress simultaneously toward
several goals in different categories. The Goals and Assessment table is
designed to support preparation of an assessment plan.

	Goal	Ongoing Assessment Opportunities	Unit Assessment Opportunities
Level I: Conceptual and Procedural Knowledge	**1.** Understand the concepts of vision line, angle, and blind spot.	**Section A** p. 4, #5 p. 6, #10 p. 8, #15 p. 9, #18	**Quiz 1** #1b, 2ab **Test** #1, 2, 5
	2. Understand the concept of glide ratio or tangent.	**Section D** p. 37, #13 p. 39, #15	**Quiz 2** #1, 3
	3. Construct and measure vision lines and blind spots (or light rays and shadows) in two- and three-dimensional representations.	**Section B** p. 19, #14	**Quiz 1** #1b, 2ab **Test** #3, 5
	4. Measure angles.	**Section B** p. 15, #6 **Section C** p. 28, #10 **Section D** p. 36, #9	**Quiz 1** #1a, 3 **Test** #8
	5. Make scale drawings of situations.	**Section B** p. 14, #4 **Section C** p. 28, #10	**Quiz 2** #3 **Test** #12

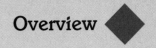

	Goal	Ongoing Assessment Opportunities	Unit Assessment Opportunities
Level II: Reasoning, Communicating, Thinking, and Making Connections	**6.** Make relative comparisons involving steepness problems.	**Section A** p. 9, #17 **Section C** p. 27, #6 **Section D** p. 34, #4c p. 35, #6 **Section E** p. 46, #2ad p. 53, #14b	**Quiz 2** #2
	7. Understand the relationship among steepness, angle, and height-to-distance ratio.	**Section A** p. 7, #12c **Section B** p. 18, #12ab **Section C** p. 28, #9 **Section D** p. 40, #23	**Test** #9, 11, 12, 13
	8. Understand the ratio between an object and its shadow caused by the sun for different times of the year.	**Section B** p. 15, #9 p. 18, #10bc	**Test** #6, 7

	Goal	Ongoing Assessment Opportunities	Unit Assessment Opportunities
Level III: Modeling, Generalizing, and Non-Routine Problem Solving	**9.** Understand the correspondence between contexts that may be represented by a right triangle.	**Section D** p. 44, For Further Reflection **Section E** p. 46, #2bc	
	10. Use ratios to solve problems.	**Section A** p. 9, #16 **Section D** p. 34, #4ab	**Test** #4, 10
	11. Solve problems using right triangle trigonometry ratios.	**Section D** p. 39, #19 **Section E** p. 49, #5b **Section E** p. 52, #13 p. 55, For Further Reflection	**Test** #9, 10, 13

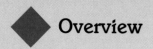

Overview

Materials Preparation

The following items are the necessary materials and resources to be used by the teacher and students throughout the unit. For further details, see the Section Overviews and the Materials section of the Hints and Comments column on each teacher page. Note: Some contexts and problems can be enhanced through the use of optional materials. These optional materials are listed in the corresponding Hints and Comments section.

Student Resources

Quantities listed are per student.
- Letter to the Family
- **Student Activity Sheets 1–10**
- **Student Activity Sheet 2** (several copies per group of students)
- **Appendix A**

Teacher Resources

No resources required

Student Materials

Quantities listed are per student, unless otherwise indicated.
- **3 ft × 5 ft length of paper (two sheets per group of students)**
- **$8\frac{1}{2}$ " × 11" paper (one sheet)**
- **Angle measure tools, constructed by students (see page 16)**
- **Books or boxes that can stand upright**
- **Calculator**
- **Centimeter cubes (at least 10 per pair of students)**
- **Centimeter ruler**
- **Cardstock**
- **Directional compass**
- **Glue (one bottle per pair of students)**
- **Markers (one per group of students)**
- **Metric measuring tape**
- **Pieces of string, straws, or uncooked spaghetti (one per pair of students)**
- **Protractors or compass cards**
- **Scissors**
- **Straightedges or rulers**
- **Sticks, 0.7 meter long**
- **Sticks, 1.2 meters long**
- **String (one roll per pair of students)**
- **Tape (one dispenser per group)**
- **Transparency with a line on it (one per student)**
- **Toy boats with flat bottoms (one per group)**

BRITANNICA

Mathematics in Context

Student Material and Teaching Notes

◆ Contents

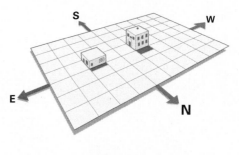

Dear Student,

Welcome to *Looking at an Angle*!

In this unit, you will learn about vision lines and blind areas. Have you ever been on one of the top floors of a tall office or apartment building? When you looked out the window, were you able to see the sidewalk directly below the building? If you could see the sidewalk, it was in your field of vision; if you could not see the sidewalk, it was in a blind spot.

The relationship between vision lines and rays of light and the relationship between blind spots and shadows are some of the topics that you will explore in this unit. Have you ever noticed how the length of a shadow varies according to the time of day? As part of an activity, you will measure the length of the shadow of a stick and the corresponding angle of the sun at different times of the day. You will then determine how the angle of the sun affects the length of a shadow.

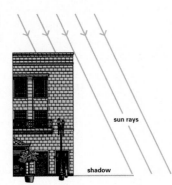

sun rays

shadow

Besides looking at the angle of the sun, you will also study the angle that a ladder makes with the floor when it is leaning against a wall and the angle that a descending hang glider makes with the ground. You will learn two different ways to identify the steepness of an object: the angle the object makes with the ground and the tangent of that angle.

We hope you enjoy discovering the many ways of "looking at an angle."

Sincerely,

The Mathematics in Context Development Team

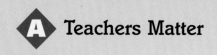 Teachers Matter

Section Focus

The instructional focus of Section A is to:

- discover the concept of vision line;
- investigate situations involving vision lines and blind spots;
- construct vision lines in two- and three-dimensional representations;
- measure angles; and
- use ratio to solve problems involving vision lines and blind spots.

Pacing and Planning

Day 1: The Grand Canyon		Student pages 1–4
INTRODUCTION	Problems 1–3	Discuss the view of the Colorado River from the rim of the Grand Canyon.
ACTIVITY	Activity, pages 2 and 3 Problem 4	Use two tables to create a model of the Grand Canyon to investigate vision lines and blind spots.
HOMEWORK	Problem 5	Write a report on the activity using the terms visible, not visible, and blind spot.

Day 2: The Table Canyon Model		Student pages 5–7
INTRODUCTION	Problems 6–9	Investigate vision lines using a diagram of the side view of the paper models.
CLASSWORK	Problems 10–12	Determine blind spots by drawing vision lines on pictures of various boats.
HOMEWORK	Problem 13	Reason about vision lines, blind spots, and driving patterns for boats.

Day 3: Ships Ahoy (Continued)		Student page 8
INTRODUCTION	Review homework.	Review homework from Day 2.
ACTIVITY	Problem 14	Determine the area of a blind spot of a toy boat.
HOMEWORK	Problem 15	Relate the size of the blind spot to the size of the boat.

Day 4: Cars and Blind Spots		Student pages 9–12
INTRODUCTION	Review homework.	Review homework from Day 3.
CLASSWORK	Problems 16–19	Discuss visions lines and blind spots of a car.
HOMEWORK	Check Your Work For Further Reflection	Student self-assessment: Identify, draw, reason about vision lines and blind spots.

Additional Resources: Additional Practice, Section A, Student Book page 56

Materials

Student Resources

Quantities listed are per student, unless otherwise noted.

- Letter to the Family
- **Student Activity Sheets 1** and **3**
- **Student Activity Sheet 2** (several copies per group of students)

Teachers Resources

No resources required

Student Materials

Quantities listed are per group of students, unless otherwise noted.

- 3' x 5' length of paper, (two sheets)
- $8\frac{1}{2}$ " x 11" paper (one sheet per student)
- Compass card or protractor (one per student)
- Marker
- Scissors (one pair per student)
- Straightedge or ruler (one per student)
- String (one roll per class)
- Tape
- Toy boat with flat bottom

* See Hints and Comments for optional materials.

Learning Lines

Informal Exploration of Steepness and Angle of Elevation

This section focuses on different contexts in which vision plays a role:

- a hiker on the rim of the Grand Canyon looking down trying to see the Colorado River;

- the captain of a ship looking at the water over the bow of the ship;
- the driver of a car looking at the road through the front windshield.

These contexts share a similar trait: there is an object blocking the view (rocks, the bow of the ship, the hood of the car). In each of these contexts, vision lines (i.e., imaginary straight lines from the eye to an object) can be used as a tool to determine what can and cannot be seen (i.e., a blind spot). Each situation can be represented with a right triangle: there is a height for the eye, an object blocking the view, a blind spot, and an angle of elevation of the vision line.

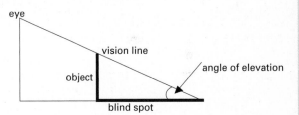

The exploration in this section is informal. Students are encouraged to discover the concept of vision line and investigate blind spots. They informally reason about the ratios involved and about the relationship with the angle between the vision line and the surface.

At the End of This Section: Learning Outcomes

Students understand the concept of vision line. They are able to construct vision lines in two- and three-dimensional representations in order to determine blind spots. They have an informal understanding of the concept of steepness and the relationship between steepness and angle of elevation.

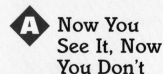
Notes

Encourage students to focus on the location of the photographer's camera, the location of the rim of the canyon, and the visibility of the river. Most students know from playing hide-and-seek that objects or persons may be hidden from view when something is in the way.

Now You See It, Now You Don't

The Grand Canyon

The Grand Canyon is one of the most famous natural wonders in the world. Located on the high plateau of northwestern Arizona, it is a huge gorge carved out by the Colorado River. It has a total length of 446 kilometers (km). Approximately 90 km of the gorge are located in the Grand Canyon National Park. The north rim of the canyon (the Kaibab Plateau) is about 2,500 meters (m) above sea level.

This photograph shows part of the Colorado River, winding along the bottom of the canyon.

1. Why can't you see the continuation of the river on the lower right side of the photo?

Reaching All Learners

Hands-On Learning

If students have difficulty with this context, you could set up a simple classroom situation to make this point clear. For example, if someone is approaching the classroom, some students may be able to see the approaching person through the open door. However, other students may find that their view of the approaching person is blocked by a wall.

Parent Involvement

Send Letter to the Family home with students. Have students share it with their parents, discussing the questions. Parents can write a comment on their experiences with the context. These letters can then be shared in class.

Solutions and Samples

1. Explanations will vary, but students should indicate that something is blocking their view. Sample student explanations:

   The ledge in front of us is hiding the Colorado River.

   The river is a long way down and the rocks are in the way.

Hints and Comments

Overview

Students look at a photograph of the Grand Canyon. They determine why the Colorado River cannot be seen in the lower right portion of the photograph.

About the Mathematics

An important mathematical goal for this section is to have students understand the concept of the vision line, an imaginary straight line from your eye to an object. Do not, however, mention this idea yet. At this point, it is enough for them to realize that something may be hidden from view because something is in the way. Later in this section, the concept of a "blind spot" will be introduced.

Planning

Students may work on problem 1 in small groups. Discuss students' answers with the class. For additional information on the Grand Canyon, visit: www.nps.gov/grca

Now You See It, Now You Don't

Notes

3 Some students may find the drawing easier to understand, while others may prefer the photograph. In either case, students should realize that the drawing simplifies the canyon's rock formations.

3 Discuss similarities as well as differences.

A Now You See It, Now You Don't

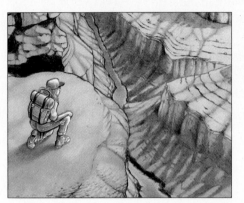

The Colorado River can barely be seen from most viewpoints in Grand Canyon National Park.

This drawing shows a hiker on the north rim overlooking a portion of the canyon.

2. Can the hiker see the river directly below her? Explain.

Here you see a photograph and a drawing of the same area of the Grand Canyon. The canyon walls are shaped like stairs in the drawing.

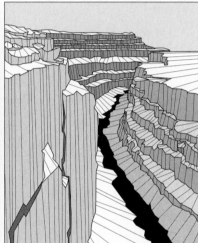

3. Describe other differences between the photo and the drawing.

Reaching All Learners

Act It Out

Students may use gestures to show how much of the canyon they will be able to see.

2 **Looking at an Angle**

Solutions and Samples

2. Answers will vary. Sample response:

   The hiker is kneeling on a rock that is blocking her view. She can probably see the river only if she looks to the left or the right.

3. Answers will vary. Sample response:

   The drawing simplifies the canyon. Details that can be seen on the photograph, such as roads, trees, differences in the color of the rock formations, and shadows, are lost in the drawing. Because these details are left out of the drawing, other features of the canyon can be seen more clearly. It is easier to see the river. It is also easier to see that the rock formations are shaped like stairs.

Hints and Comments

Overview

Students visualize how much of the Colorado River a hiker on the rim can see. Students also consider the difference between a drawing and a photograph of the Grand Canyon.

About the Mathematics

In problem 1, students were asked to work with information supplied by a photograph. Problem 2 is different in the sense that students have to put themselves in the position of the hiker to imagine this person's view of the river. Problem 2 is aiming at the idea of vision lines. Students may actually come up with the idea of using string or something else to show such a line.

Planning

Students may work on problems 2 and 3 in small groups. You may want to discuss students' answers with the whole class.

The Table Canyon Model

In this activity, you will build your own "table canyon" to investigate how much of the "river" can be seen from different perspectives. To do this activity, you will need at least three people: two viewers and one recorder.

Materials
- two tables
- two large sheets of paper
- a meter stick
- markers
- a boat (optional)

Be sure each student gets the chance to sit behind the table.

- Place two tables parallel to each other, with enough room between them for another table to fit.

- Hang large sheets of paper from the tables to the floor as shown in the photograph above. The paper represents the canyon walls, and the floor between the two tables represents the river.

- Sit behind one of the tables, and have a classmate sit behind the other. Each of you is viewing the canyon from a different perspective.

- Have another classmate mark the lowest part of the canyon wall visible to each of you viewing the canyon. The recorder should make at least three marks along each canyon wall.

Reaching All Learners

Extension

To give students experiences with different perspectives and vision lines, have the students stand up or use different size tables.

Hints and Comments

Materials

3 ft × 5 ft length of paper (two sheets per group
of students);
markers (one per group of students);
string (one roll per group of students);
scissors (one pair per student or group of students);
tape (one roll per group of students);
toy boats with flat bottoms, optional (one per group
of students)

Overview

Students build their own canyons out of tables and
paper. They investigate the boundaries of what they
can and cannot see. They use their results to answer
questions on page 4.

About the Mathematics

Students should discover the idea of vision lines in
answering the problems on Student Book pages 1–3.
The eye is used as the starting point of the vision line
while the dot placed on the opposite canyon wall is
the ending point. Informally, students investigate
angle of elevation, steepness, and blind spots.

Planning

Each student in the group should have a different
color marker.

When students construct their model canyons, make
sure that the sheets of paper representing the canyon
walls are hanging straight down to the floor. Also,
make sure that every student gets to sit in a chair and
investigate vision lines.

A Now You See It, Now You Don't

Notes

4 If students have difficulty, you might have them represent the line from each student's eyes to each of the three marks with string.

4e and f You may wish to have students experiment using a toy boat. Students may put the boat in several different places. For example, they could put it in a visible area and move it closer and closer toward a canyon wall until it disappears from view.

Discuss what makes the two drawings similar.

Measure the height of the marks from the floor with the meter stick, and make notes for a report so that you can answer the following.

4. **a.** Can either of you see the river below? Explain.

b. On which wall are the marks higher, yours or your classmate's? Explain.

c. Are all the marks on one wall the same height? Explain.

d. What are some possible changes that would allow you to see the river better? Predict how each change affects what you can see.

e. Where would you place a boat on the river so that both of you can see it?

f. What would change if the boat were placed closer to one of the canyon walls?

5. Write a report on this activity describing your investigations and discoveries. You may want to use the terms *visible, not visible,* and *blind spot* in your report.

These drawings show two schematic views of the canyon. The one on the right looks something like the table canyon from the previous activity.

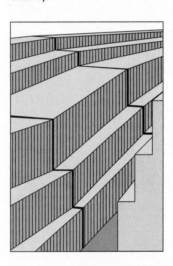
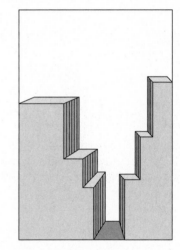

Assessment Pyramid

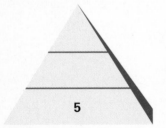

Understand the concept of blind spot.

Reaching All Learners

English Language Learners

Be sure students understand the terms *visible* and *blind spot*. These may not be part of their usual vocabulary.

Writing Opportunity/Parent Involvement

You may ask students to write their answers to problem 5 in their journals. Writing a report on this activity encourages students to reflect on what they did, and gives you something to refer to during the rest of the unit. Students can share their report with their parents and have parents share a blind spot experience, which can be added to the report.

Solutions and Samples

4. a. Answers will vary, depending on the sitting height of the student, how far s/he leans toward the edge, and the distance between the tables. A taller person or a person leaning towards the edge has a better chance of seeing the river.

b. Answers will vary. The marks of a taller student will be lower down the canyon, unless a shorter student leans closer to the edge of the canyon.

c. Yes. Explanations will vary. Sample explanation:

The marks on the opposite wall should all be at the same height because the table position determines how far down I can look. I can even move my head up and down; it doesn't depend on the height of my eyes but on the blocked view from the table edge. If the tables were not parallel, the marks would not be at the same height; I would see farther down the canyon where the tables were farther apart.

d. Answers will vary. Sample response:

There are several things I can do to see the river. I can sit up straight, stand up, lean forward, or widen the canyon by moving one or both tables.

e. Answers will vary. Sample responses:

If we could both see just enough of the river to see the middle, then we could see a boat coming down the middle of the river.

If the boat was farther down the river, to the right or left of us, both of us could see it.

f. Answers will vary. Sample response:

If the boat moved closer to one of the canyon walls, then whoever was sitting next to that wall would no longer be able to see the boat. The edge of the table blocked the view of the river from the person sitting there.

5. Reports will vary. Sample report:

I was surprised that the marks I could see were all at the same height. We decide this was because the tables were parallel and the edge of the table blocked views of the canyon. At first, the river was not visible at all. Then we moved the tables farther apart so that the opposite side of the river was visible. When the boat came down my side of the river, it was in my blind spot, and it didn't matter how far up or down the river the boat was. The boat became visible to me only when it moved to the other side of the river or far to my left or right.

Hints and Comments

Overview

Students continue working on the activity from page 3 and answer problems related to the activity.

Planning

Students may work on problem 4 in small groups or as a class. They may work on problem 5 individually. At the end of the activity, have students discuss their results with the whole class.

Comments About the Solutions

4. c. This problem can lead to an interesting discussion because the results may not be what students expected. Some students may have expected the mark in the middle to be lower than those on the sides, thinking that the "shortest route" would allow them to see further down the wall.

A Now You
See It, Now
You Don't

Notes

6 and 8 Students can use the line on the transparency as vision line.

7 Students may need help using the scale to determine the height of the canyon.

9 Students may need to draw the vision lines to see which ledge is blocking the view.

We will look more closely at that drawing on the right. Now we see it in a scale drawing of the *cross-section* of the canyon.

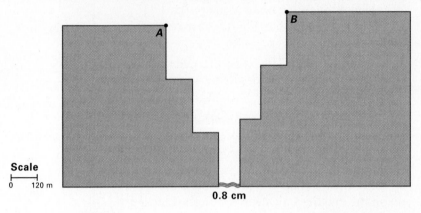

Scale
0   120 m

0.8 cm

6. Is it possible to see the river from point A on the left rim? Why or why not?

7. What is the actual height of the left canyon wall represented in the scale drawing?

8. If the river were 1.2 centimeters (cm) wide in the scale drawing, could it be seen from point A?

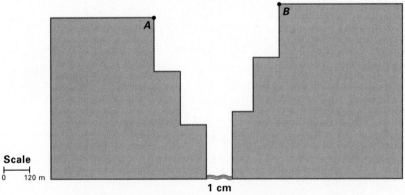

Scale
0   120 m

1 cm

9. In the scale drawing above, the river is now 1 cm wide. Is it possible to see the river from point B? If not, which ledge is blocking your view? Explain.

Reaching All Learners

Accommodation

Have copies of the drawing for students so they can mark it as they go. Some students may wish to cut these out so they can move the canyons.

Vocabulary Building

Students may need a reminder about cross sections. Have a discussion about when they've used this term in science class.

Extension

Explain why wide canyon ledges make it difficult to see the river.

Solutions and Samples

6. No. Explanations will vary. Sample explanation:

It is not possible to see the river from point A, because when I use a ruler as a vision line, it hits the opposite canyon wall, as shown below. The result is the same as in the Table Canyon Activity.

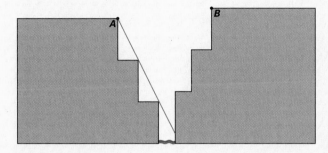

7. The actual height is 720 meters. Point A is six centimeters above the river in the model. Every centimeter in the drawing represents 120 meters. In a ratio table:

	× 6	
Drawing	1 cm	6 cm
Reality	120 m	720 m

8. Yes. More of the river can be seen. A vision line to at least part of the river is now clear. Students may check by measuring how far the vision line would meet the river level from the left wall. This distance is less than 1.2 cm.

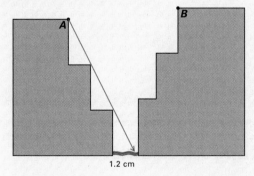

1.2 cm

9. No. The first ledge below point B blocks the line of sight, as shown below.

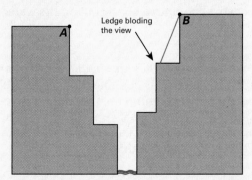

Ledge bloding the view

Hints and Comments

Materials

calculators, optional (one per student);
centimeter rulers (one per student);
a transparency with a line of about 10 cm long
  (one transparency per student)

Overview

Students study schematic representations of the Grand Canyon. Students work on problems involving scale and ratio. The problems are related to a cross section of the canyon.

About the Mathematics

The photograph of the Grand Canyon shown on page 2 is being schematized more and more, first to the drawing on page 2, then on page 4 to perspective drawings with less and less details, and finally to a cross section as shown on page 5. Students should be familiar with drawing and interpreting cross sections. They have to realize that a vision line starts from point A and extends straight until it meets with something opaque. Students should also have a basic understanding of scale and ratio. They should be familiar with the use of a ratio table.

Planning

You may discuss with students what information is represented in a cross section that is to scale. Students may work on problems 6–9 in small groups. You may want to discuss problems 6 and 7 in class.

Comments About the Solutions

6.–9.
Encourage students to use a ratio table to solve the scale problems. You may also wish to have them use a calculator.

8. Students may make a scale drawing representing a canyon with a wider river.

A **Now You See It, Now You Don't**

Notes

10 After answering this problem, ask students how this relates to the canyon context.

Students may need help making sense of the terms "vision line" and "field of vision".

Ships Ahoy

Picture yourself in a small rowboat rowing toward a ship that is tied to a dock. In the first picture, the captain at the helm of the ship is able to see you. As you get closer, at some point the captain is no longer able to see you.

10. Explain why the captain cannot see you in the fourth picture.

The captain's height and position in the ship determine what the captain can and cannot see in front of the ship. The shape of the ship will also affect his field of vision. To find the captain's field of vision, you can draw a **vision line**. A vision line is an imaginary line that extends from the captain's eyes, over the edge of the ship, and to the water.

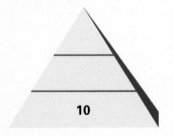

Assessment Pyramid

10

Understand the concept of blind spot.

Reaching All Learners

Intervention

If students have difficulty, you might remind them of the Canyon Table Model Activity, where they moved a boat into a blind spot on the water by bringing it closer to a canyon wall.

Extension

Ask students, *Is it true that if you cannot see the captain, the captain cannot see you?* (This statement is true.) However, it is possible that you are able to see the captain's head sticking out but you cannot see the captain's eyes. In that case, the captain cannot see your eyes. So if you cannot see the captain's eyes, the captain cannot see your eyes. For this reason, in traffic, people often try to make eye contact with other drivers.

Solutions and Samples

10. Explanations will vary. Sample explanations:

I cannot see the captain, so he cannot see me.

As I row, I move closer to the ship. It's just like in the Table Canyon Model Activity. When the boat was close to my side of the canyon, I couldn't see it. When I get closer to the ship, the captain cannot see me because the ship's bow is blocking his view.

Hints and Comments

Overview

Students investigate the blind spot of a captain standing on the bridge of a ship. The concept of a vision line is made explicit.

About the Mathematics

Again we are dealing with a person looking at something with his or her view partially obstructed by an object (in this case the bow of the boat). On the next page, students will draw vision lines, measure the angle the vision line makes with the water, and draw conclusions about the captain's blind spot. Later in this section, blind spot will be referred to as the "blind area."

Planning

Before students begin problem 10, you may want to introduce some nautical terms, such as *bow*, *stern*, *bridge*, *crew*, and *sail*. Students may work on problem 10 in small groups.

Did You Know?

A ship has two main sections—the front, or bow, and the back, or stern. A ship is navigated from a raised platform called the bridge. Some ships have a sail, which is a piece of fabric that, with the wind, propels the ship through water. The people who work on a ship are the crew.

A Now You See It, Now You Don't

Notes

Students must know how to use a protractor to complete this activity. Some review may be needed.

11 Rulers are necessary for drawing straight vision lines. Students should also extend the bottom of the boats to help measure the angles. Also, if students reason that there are other obstacles on the boat that are in the way, such as towers, tell them that the captain can see past those.

11. For each ship shown on **Student Activity Sheet 1**, draw a vision line from the captain, over the front edge of the ship, to the water. Measure the angle between the vision line and the water. (A star marks the captain's location.)

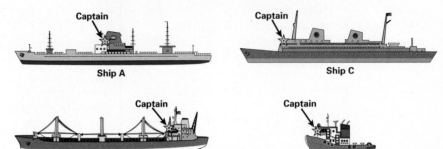

12. Compare the ships on **Student Activity Sheet 1**.

   a. On which ship is the captain's blind area the smallest? Explain.

   b. How does the shape of the ship affect the captain's view?

   c. How does the angle between the vision line and the water affect the captain's view?

Suppose that you are swimming in the water and a large boat is coming toward you. If you are too close to the boat, the captain may not be able to see you! In order to see a larger area of the water, a captain can travel in a zigzag course.

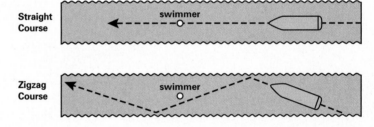

13 Students may make top-view or side-view drawings or use words to explain why the captain has a better chance of seeing the swimmer by traveling a zigzag course. Students should refer to vision lines and blind spots.

13. Explain why the captain has a better chance of seeing something in front of the boat by traveling in a zigzag course.

Assessment Pyramid

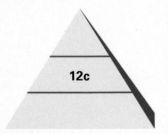

Understand the relationship between the angle and the height-to-distance ratio.

Reaching All Learners

Intervention

If students have difficulty, you might have them model the situation with a toy boat. Have students use a string to model the vision line.

Accommodation

Some students may need an enlarged copy of the Straight and Zigzag Courses.

Solutions and Samples

11.

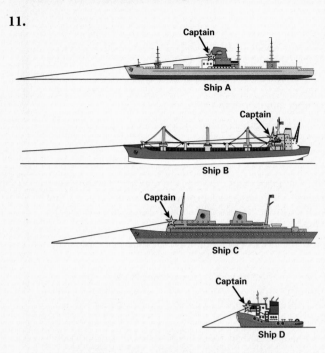

Ship A

Ship B

Ship C

Ship D

The angles of the vision lines are approximately as follows:

Ship A: 6°   Ship C: 10°

Ship B: 3°   Ship D: 23°

12. a. The captain of Ship D has the smallest blind area and the best view.

b. Explanations will vary. Sample explanation:

On Ship D, the captain's bridge is close to the bow and very high. The captain's vision line is steeper than those of the captains on the other ships.

On Ship B, the captain's bridge is at the back of the ship. The vision line extends a long way and is more horizontal than those of the captains on the other ships. The captain of Ship B has the biggest blind spot and the worst visibility.

c. Explanations will vary. Sample explanation:

On Ship D, the angle between the vision line and the water is large, and the blind spot is small.

On Ship B, the angle between the vision line and the water is very small, and the blind spot is large. When the angle is large, there is a small blind spot and good visibility, and when the angle is small, there is a large blind spot and poor visibility.

Hints and Comments

Materials

Student Activity Sheet 1 (one per student); straightedges (one per student); compass cards or protractors (one per student); string, optional (one roll per group); toy boats with flat bottoms, optional (one per group)

Overview

Students draw vision lines and measure the angle between the vision line and the water. They draw conclusions about the size of the captain's field of vision. Students also investigate how sailing a zigzag course changes the captain's field of vision.

Planning

Students may work on problems 11 and 12 in small groups. Discuss students' answers in class. You might review how to measure angles with a compass card, which is introduced in the unit *Figuring All the Angles*. Students may work on problem 13 individually or in small groups. This problem is optional. If time is a concern, it may be omitted or assigned as homework. If you assign problem 13 as homework, be sure to discuss students' answers in class.

Comments About the Solutions

11. Students' angle measurements will vary due to errors in measurement. Accept responses that are close to the given angle measurements in the Solutions column.

13. Explanations may vary. Sample response:

By zigzagging, the captain is no longer looking over the bow of the boat, but over the side. The side of the ship is closer to the bridge, so the captain's vision line over the side of the ship is steeper and provides a better view than the vision line over the bow. The drawings below show why:

If the captain sails straight ahead, the swimmer is in the boat's blind spot.

If the captain turns the boat, the swimmer is out of the blind spot.

Notes

Before the activity
Make sure that students understand what a blind spot is (the area of water that the captain cannot see). You may want to have a class discussion about area and how to determine the area of partial squares. Remind students to think of strategies they used in the unit *Reallotment*.

14 Discuss and make predictions before doing the activity.

15 Students should realize that they must make a fair comparison. They must determine which boat has the largest or smallest blind spot relative to its size. A chart would be helpful. See solutions.

Activity

For this activity, each group of students needs a piece of string and a toy boat. The boat can be made of either plastic or wood, but it must have a flat bottom.

Line up all the boats in the front of the classroom. For each boat, assign a number and determine the captain's location.

14. Without measuring, decide which boat has the largest blind spot and which has the smallest blind spot. Explain your decisions.

When comparing blind spots, you have to take into account the size of the boat. A large boat will probably have a large blind spot, but you must consider the size of the blind spot relative to the size of the boat.

In your group, use the following method to measure your boat's blind spot.

Place your boat on the **Student Activity Sheet 2** graph paper. Trace the bottom of the boat. Attach a piece of string to the boat at the place where the captain is located. The string represents the captain's vision line.

Using the string and a pencil, mark the spot on the graph paper where the captain's vision line hits the water. Make sure the vision line is stretched taut and touches the edge of the boat.

Mark several places on the graph paper where the captain's vision line hits the water so that you can determine the shape of the blind spot (the captain looks straight ahead and sideways). If the graph paper is not large enough, tape several pieces together. Draw the blind spot on the graph paper.

Find the area of the blind spot. Note: Each square on the graph paper is one square centimeter.

15. Make a list of the data for each boat. Decide which boat has the largest blind spot relative to its size and which has the smallest blind spot relative to its size.

Assessment Pyramid

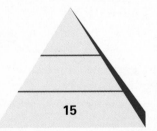

Understand the concept of blind spot.

Reaching All Learners

Intervention

Add a column that would show the ratio of the area of the boat to the area of the blind spot to the chart for problem 15. Convert the ratios to decimals. *What would a ratio of 1 mean?* Students may have an easier time if it's referenced as a ratio of one, equal to one, or greater than one.

Accommodation

Read through the activity and prepare a bullet summary of the directions.

Solutions and Samples

14. Estimates and explanations will vary. Students may base their explanations on the following features.

- The position of the bridge—a captain at the back of the boat will probably see less.

- The height of the bridge—a high bridge will improve visibility.

- The height of the bow or side of the boat—if the obstacle blocking the captain's view is high, the captain will see less.

- Some boats may have other obstacles besides the bow that block the captain's view.

15. Tables and rankings will vary. Students should give their data in square centimeters. Sample table:

Boat	Area of the Blind Spot (in cm²)	Area of the Boat (in cm²)
1	55	44
2	91	68
3	94	64
4	56	192
5	844	176
6	140	136
7	237	60
8	754	56

In the sample table above, Boats 1 and 4 have blind spots that are similar in size. Students should look at the size of the boat. Boat 1 is much smaller, which means it has a relatively larger blind spot.

Two possible strategies to make the comparisons:

- Divide both the area of each boat's blind spot and the area of the boat by the area of the boat. As a result, the area of the boat becomes 1, making it possible to compare the boats fairly, as shown below.

Boat	Area of Blind Spot (in boat units)	Area of Boat (in boat units)
1	1.25	1
2	1.34	1
3	1.47	1
and so on		

Encourage students to use a calculator. Discuss with students how many decimal points they need and how to round off.

Hints and Comments

Materials

Student Activity Sheet 2 (several copies per group); string (one roll per group); scissors (one per student); tape (one dispenser per group); toy boats with flat bottoms (one per group)

Overview

Students estimate the relative sizes of the blind spots of different toy boats. They check their estimates by measuring the blind spots. Students make a list of the data for the boats and draw conclusions about the sizes of the blind spots relative to the sizes of the boats.

Planning

Students may work on problems 14 and 15 in small groups. The activity will take an entire class period. The activity will work better if students have different-sized boats. If boats are not available, try using cars or other toy vehicles. Discuss students' results.

Comments About the Solutions

14. You may wish to discuss with students whether the water underneath the boat should be considered part of the blind spot as well. (In the steps listed in the Student Book, the area underneath the boat is not considered part of the blind spot.)

Also, it must be clear in what direction the captain is looking. It is possible to have the captain look in all directions, but you may want to narrow this down to have the captain look straight ahead and sideways only (the steps listed in the Student Book are based on the assumption that the captain looks only straight ahead and to the side.)

- Look at the ratio between the area of the blind spot and the area of the boat as shown above. For instance, for Boat 1 the ratio is 1.25:1. In other words, the area of the blind spot is 1.25 times as big as the area of the boat. This approach is basically the same as the first, but the reasoning is slightly different.

A | Now You
See It, Now
You Don't

Notes

16 Students should make a fair comparison by relating the length of the blind area to the length of the car. When discussing, have students measure how many car lengths long the blind spot is. This will make problem 17 easier to understand.

18 Clarify that the vision line is from the driver's eyes looking up from the top of the windshield.

19 You may want to discuss students' answers in class. Check students' work for appropriate mathematical language, appropriateness of the pictures, and originality of context. In most cases, a top-view drawing will not be appropriate because it shows in which direction you are looking, but does not indicate the area you cannot see.

Cars and Blind Spots

This photograph is of a 1958 Pontiac Star Chief. This car is 5.25 m long.

Here is a side view of the car with vision lines indicating the blind area.

Today cars are designed so that the blind area in front of the car is much smaller. The car shown below is a 1997 Buick Skylark that is 4.7 m long. Notice how the vision line touches the hood of this car.

16. Find the length of road in front of each car that cannot be seen by the driver.

17. Which car has the longest relative blind spot?

18. What does the vision line that extends upward from each car indicate? Why is it important that this vision line be as close to vertical as possible?

19. Describe a situation from your daily life which involves a blind spot. Include a drawing of the situation with the blind spot clearly indicated.

Assessment Pyramid

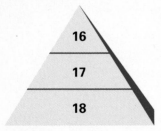

Use ratios to solve problems involving steepness, make relative comparisons, and understand vision angles.

Reaching All Learners

Intervention

If students are confused about how to start problem 16, ask them to point out the part of the road that cannot be seen by the driver.

Extension

How are the blind spots in cars influenced by the height of the drivers?

Parent Involvement

Use problem 19 as homework for students to discuss with their parents. Challenge them to develop a situation other than one discussed in class.

You might have students measure the length of the blind area of their family car, a bicycle, or a motorcycle. All the data can then be compared in class.

Solutions and Samples

16. Pontiac 10 m, Buick, 3.5 m. Estimates can vary. Students may use a variety of strategies to find their answers. Sample strategy:

Cut a strip of paper and use it to mark the length of the Pontiac, bumper to bumper. The length of the Pontiac is 5.25 meters, so the length represented on the strip of paper must also be 5.25 meters. The strip fits in the length of the blind area almost two times. Therefore, the length of the blind area must be about 10 meters, as shown here.

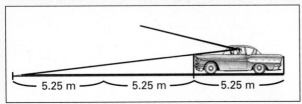

— 5.25 m — 5.25 m — 5.25 m —

Mark the length of the Buick on another strip of paper. The length represented on the strip is 4.7 meters. The strip fits in the length of the blind area less than once. So, the length of the blind area is about 3.5 meters, as shown here.

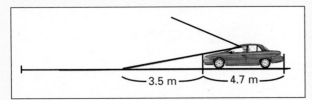

— 3.5 m — 4.7 m —

17. The Pontiac. The blind area of the Pontiac is about twice as long as the car. The blind area of the Buick is less than the length of the car. So the Pontiac has a relatively longer blind spot.

18. Answers will vary. Sample response:

This vision line indicates what the driver can and cannot see when looking up. It is important that this line be as steep as possible so that the driver can see high traffic lights.

19. Answers will vary. Sample responses:

• If I want to see the cat, I cannot see it if I'm standing behind the chair, because the chair is between us.

Hints and Comments

Materials

scissors (one pair per student); $8\frac{1}{2}$" × 11" paper (one sheet per student)

Overview

Students compare the lengths of the blind areas of two different cars. Students also describe a situation from their daily lives involving a blind spot.

About the Mathematics

The idea of a vision angle is implied in problem 18. There are an infinite number of vision lines you can draw between objects that define the field of vision. The crucial vision lines for the car indicate what the driver can see in front of the car. Both vision lines form an angle.

Planning

Students may work on problems 16–19 individually. Problems 16–18 are optional. Discuss students' answers in class.

The last example in the Solutions column shows the drawings of a student who is struggling with this concept. The student added the side and front views only after feedback from the teacher.

• When I'm working at my desk, and I look sideways, there is a large area of the floor I cannot see.

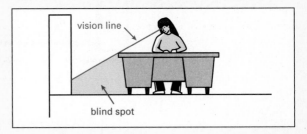

vision line

blind spot

• When I wake up in the morning, I cannot see the floor next to my bed because the edge of my bed is blocking my view.

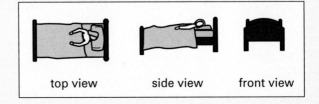

top view   side view   front view

Notes

Summary

Have students share their
responses to problem 19
with class. When reading
the Summary, refer to
situations discussed
dealing with these terms.

 Now You See It, Now You Don't

Summary

When an object is hidden from your view because something is in
the way, the area that you cannot see is called the **blind area** or
blind spot.

Vision lines are imaginary lines that go from a person's eyes to an
object. Vision lines show what is in a person's line of sight, and they
can be used to determine whether or not an object is visible.

In this section, you used vision lines to discover that the Colorado
River is not visible in some parts of the Grand Canyon. You also used
vision lines to find the captain's blind area for ships of various sizes.

Check Your Work

These drawings on **Student Activity Sheet 3** show three different ways
a ship's bridge, or steering house, can be positioned. The dot on each
boat is the front of the boat.

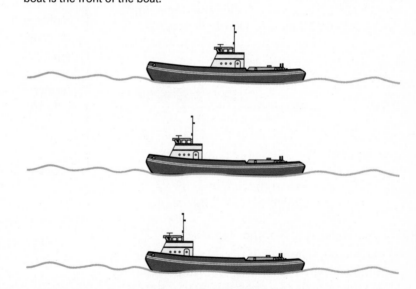

Reaching All Learners

Vocabulary Building

Be sure students recognize that the horizon is horizontal!

Hints and Comments

Overview

Students read the Summary, which reviews the main concepts covered in this section. Students use the Check Your Work problems as self-assessment. The answers to these problems are also provided on pages 61 and 62 of the Student Book. After students complete Section A, you may assign as homework appropriate activities from the Additional Practice section, located on Student Book page 56.

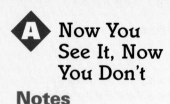

**Now You
See It, Now
You Don't**

Notes

1. **a.** Draw the visions lines to show the blind spots of the captain in each of the three cases.

   b. Measure the angle between the vision line and the horizon in each case.

   c. How does the blind spot at the back of ship change if you move the bridge forward?

Vision lines, such as the ones you drew on **Student Activity Sheet 1**, do not show everything that captains can and cannot see. For example, some ships' bridges, the area from which the captain navigates the ship, are specially constructed to improve the captain's view. The captain can walk across the bridge, from one side of the boat to the other side, to increase his or her field of vision.

Below is a photograph of a large cruise ship. Notice how the bridge, located between the arrows, has wings that project out on each side of the ship.

2. Explain how the wings of the bridge give the captain a better view of the water in front of the ship.

Assessment Pyramid

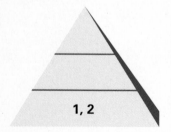

1, 2

Assesses Section A Goals

Reaching All Learners

Extension

If the best spot for the bridge is near the front of the boat, what happens when the boat moves in reverse?

11 Looking at an Angle

Solutions and Samples

Answers to Check Your Work

1. a.

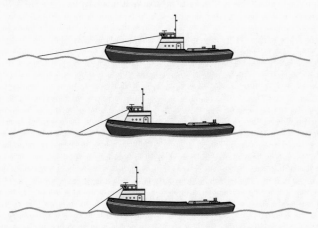

b. 8°–10°

20°

30°

c. The blind spot gets smaller in front but larger in back.

2. The captain can walk to the ends of the wings and increase the area he or she can see directly in front and on the sides of the ship. You can make a drawing showing how the blind spot moves as the captain walks from one side of the bridge to the other, as shown here.

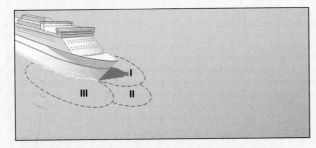

Area I indicates the blind spot when standing on the left side of the bridge.

Area II indicates the blind spot when standing in the middle of the bridge.

Area III indicates the blind spot when standing on the right side of the bridge.

Hints and Comments

Materials

straightedges (one per student);
Student Activity Sheet 3 (one per student);
compass cards or protractors (one per student)

Overview

Students draw vision lines and measure the angle between the vision line and the water. They draw conclusions about the size of the captain's blind spot. Students also study a boat with a wing-like bridge to improve the captain's view.

Planning

These problems may be used for student self-assessment.

 **A** Section

Hydrofoils have fins that raise the boat out of the water when it travels at high speeds.

3. Make two side-view drawings of a hydrofoil: one of the hydrofoil in the water traveling at slow speed and one of it rising out of the water and traveling at high speed. Use vision lines to show the difference between the captain's view in each drawing. (You may design your own hydrofoil.)

▣ For Further Reflection

When you approach a town from afar, you sometimes see a tall tower or building. As you move closer to the town, the tall object seems to disappear. Make a drawing with vision lines to show why the tower or building seem to disappear when you get closer to town.

For Further Reflection

You may need to encourage students to get started by drawing a sketch of a town with a tall building and some smaller buildings as well. Remind them to choose an appropriate view (top, side, or front) to draw the situation in order to explain the phenomenon of the disappearing tall building. Tell students it is okay if they need several trial sketches.

Assessment Pyramid

□ FFR

3

Assesses Section A Goals

Reaching All Learners

Intervention

If students have difficulty with problem 3, you might prepare two transparencies: one showing a hydrofoil and a vision line and one showing the water level. Moving the transparency with the hydrofoil up from the water will help students see what happens: the vision line stays the same, the angle between the vision line and the water stays the same, but the blind spot increases.

Solutions and Samples

3. Your drawings may differ from the ones shown here.

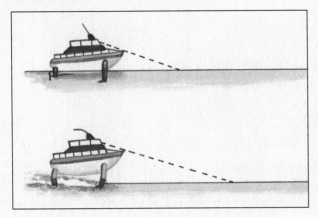

The higher the ship, the larger the captain's blind spot.

For Further Reflection

Answers will vary. Student drawings should include vision lines. A sample side-view drawing:

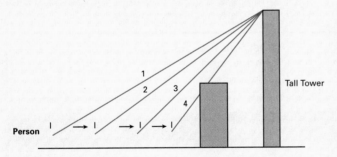

A person is moving toward a tall tower. The lines with numbers represent vision lines from the person looking at the top of the tall tower. Vision lines 1, 2, and 3 show that from those positions the person can still see the top of the tower; vision line 4 indicates that the person at that point cannot see the top of the tower anymore. There is another building blocking the view.

Hints and Comments

Materials

straightedges (one per student);
blank transparencies, optional (two per class)

Overview

Students study a hydrofoil that is lifted from the water at high speeds.

About the Mathematics

Students imagine themselves on the bridge of the boat to discover the area the captain cannot see in front of the boat. Sketching the situation can be helpful. Students may first think that their view will improve as the boat lifts out of the water, since this was the case with the previous boats: a boat with a tall bridge gives the captain a better view. However, it is not just the captain that is lifted, but also the whole boat, causing the bow to block even more of the area in front of the boat.

Planning

Problem 3 may be used for students' self-assessment.

Section Focus

The instructional focus of Section B is to:

- explore the movement of the sun throughout the day and for different seasons;
- investigate the length of shadows caused by the sun, in relation to the steepness of the sun's rays;
- measure angles;
- use ratios to solve problems involving light rays and shadows;
- construct shadows in two- and three-dimensional representations;
- compare shadows caused by the sun with shadows caused by a nearby light source; and
- discover how vision lines are similar to light rays.

Pacing and Planning

Day 5: Shadows and the Sun		Student pages 13–15
INTRODUCTION	Problems 1 and 2	Investigate changes in shadows cast by the sun.
CLASSWORK	Problems 3–8	Create a table and scale drawings relating the direction of the sun, the length of shadows, and the angle of the sun's rays for different times of the day.
HOMEWORK	Problem 9	Describe the changes in the length of a shadow and the angle of the sun's rays from season to season.

Day 6: Shadows and the Sun (Continued)		Student pages 16–18
ACTIVITY	Activity, pages 16 and 17	Conduct an experiment to compare the length and angle of shadows from the sun at different times throughout the day.
HOMEWORK	Problems 10–12	Analyze the results of the shadows from the sun experiment.

Day 7: Shadows Cast by the Sun and Lights		Student pages 18–21
INTRODUCTION	Review homework.	Review homework from Day 6.
CLASSWORK	Problems 13–16	Sketch and describe differences between shadows caused by a nearby light source and the sun.
ACTIVITY	Activity, page 21	Begin an investigation of blind areas for a model of a tugboat.

Day 8: A Shadow is a Blind Spot		Student pages 21–24
ACTIVITY	Activity, page 21	Complete the investigation of blind areas for a model of a tugboat.
CLASSWORK	Check Your Work	Student self-assessment: Identify and draw blind spots and shadows cast by the sun.
HOMEWORK	For Further Reflection	Define key terms from Sections A and B.

Day 9: Summary		
INTRODUCTION	Review	Review classwork and homework from Day 9.
ASSESSMENT	Quiz 1	Assessment of Section A and B Goals.

Additional Resources: Additional Practice, Section B, Student Book page 57

Materials

Student Resources

Quantities listed are per student.

- **Student Activity Sheets 4–9**

Teachers Resources

No resources required

Student Materials

Quantities listed are per pair of students, unless otherwise noted.

- Angle measure tools constructed by students on Student page 16
- Construction paper (one sheet per student)
- Glue
- Magnetic (directional) compass
- Metric measuring tape
- Protractor and/or compass card
- Scissors
- Stick, 0.7 meter long
- Stick, 1.2 meters long
- Straightedge or ruler
- String (one roll per class)
- centimeter cubes (one per pair of students)

* See Hints and Comments for optional materials.

Learning Lines

Spatial Sense

The mathematical content of this section is presented in the context of shadows. A typical real world context becomes a rich source for students to develop geometrical concepts, contributing to their spatial sense. Students have undoubtedly encountered real life phenomena concerning light and shadow earlier. Now they learn to discuss these phenomena in mathematical terms, learning to reason about them and draw conclusions based on mathematical representations, visualizations and systematic exploration.

At the End of This Section: Learning Outcomes

Students understand how shadows are similar to blind spots. They can construct shadows, both caused by the sun or by a nearby light source, in two- and three-dimensional representations. Students develop a broader and deeper understanding of the concepts of steepness and angle of elevation.

Shadows and Blind Spots

Notes

Start the class with a discussion of shadows and sunlight. Ask students what they know about topics such as:

- the relation between shadows' directions and the direction the sun is shining from;
- the relation between the length of a shadow and the object casting the shadow;
- the sun's movement in the sky during the day;
- the varying length of shadows during a day, or during a year; and so on.
- the difference in sun shadows for those living in the Northern and Southern hemispheres.

1 Have graph paper available for students. Have them show answers on the overheard.

2 Discuss why the 9 A.M. shadow is not 2 meters long. (The diagonal is longer than a side of a square.)

Shadows and Blind Spots

Shadows and the Sun

When the sun is shining, it casts shadows. The length of the shadow varies throughout the day. Sometimes shadows are very short (when the sun is "high"), and sometimes they are very long (when the sun is rising or setting).

  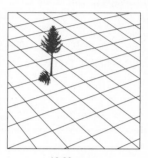

6:00 A.M.   9:00 A.M.   12:00 NOON

Here are three sketches of a tree and its shadow in the early morning, mid-morning, and noon.

1. Sketch how the pictures would look at 3.00 P.M. and 6.00 P.M.

The tree is two meters high. The tiles are one meter wide.

2. At what time do you think the tree's shadow will be two meters long?

The sun rises in the east.

3. Indicate east, west, north, and south in your sketch.

Reaching All Learners

Intervention

Talk about where the directions (east, west, north, and south) would be located on the picture in the book. This will help students answer problem 2.

Accommodation

Students can use cm graph paper to draw the top views of the shadows at 6, 9, and 12 A.M. If students have difficulty with this activity, complete this using a copy of graph paper on a transparency. Then students can draw the shadows for problem 1 on the same paper.

Solutions and Samples

1. At 3 P.M.:

3:00 P.M.

At 6 P.M.:

6:00 P.M.

2. The shadow will be around 2 meters at around 10 A.M. (and around 2 P.M.).

3.

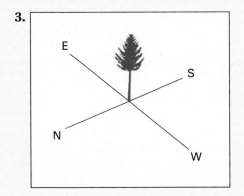

Hints and Comments

Materials

centimeter graph paper, optional (one sheet per student)

Overview

Students start their investigation of shadows. The first part of this section deals with shadows caused by the sun.

About the Mathematics

A blind spot (or blind area) is a region not seen by someone; a shadow (or shaded area) is a region not reached by light rays. In both cases, there is an object that is blocking the "view." In the context of trees, vision lines cannot go through a tree, and neither can light rays.

Planning

You may want to start this section with a class discussion about shadows caused by the sun. This will give you an opportunity to investigate students' informal knowledge of shadows. Students will have gathered this knowledge from daily life observations, but it is likely they have not systematized what they know nor investigated their observations from a mathematical viewpoint. Before starting this section, students can observe the length and direction of shadows in relation to the sun's position in the sky.

Comments About the Solutions

1.–3.
   Encourage students to closely examine the three sketches of the tree's shadow, focusing on the changes in shadow length and direction. They should also realize that the sun is shining from the direction opposite the direction the shadow points at. You also may need to remind students that the sun rises in the east, sets in the west, and travels across the southern part of the sky.

2. An estimation based on the three given sketches is sufficient.

B Shadows and Blind Spots

Notes

It is key to point out that the shadow for any twelve-hour span (for example, 6 A.M. and 6 P.M.) will be the same length and along the same line but opposite directions from the tree.

Having centimeter graph paper available is helpful.

Here is a table to organize and record information.

Time of Day	Direction of Sun	Length of Shadow	Angle of Sun's Ray
6:00 A.M.	E	5 m	?
9:00 A.M.			
12:00 P.M.			

In order to find the angle of the sun's rays, you can make a scale drawing of a right triangle showing the 2-m tree and the length of the shadow. You can then use your protractor or compass card to measure the angle of the sun's ray.

Here is a scale drawing for the 6:00 A.M. picture.

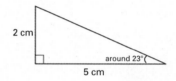

4 Ask students what happens if their drawings are not drawn to scale.

4. Use the pictures on the previous page to create scale drawings for the two remaining pictures. Use this information to copy and complete the table.

5 The angle of the sun's rays can be measured after making the scale drawings.

5. Fill in the values for 3:00 P.M. and 6:00 P.M., assuming that the sun is at the highest point at noon.

Assessment Pyramid

Make scale drawings of situations.

Reaching All Learners

Vocabulary Building

A right triangle is a triangle with a right angle. The tree is the height, the shadow is the distance, and together these two "sides" form the right angle.

Intervention

To find the length of the shadow for 9 A.M., have students draw a 2 cm × 2 cm square and measure along the diagonal.

Solutions and Samples

4.

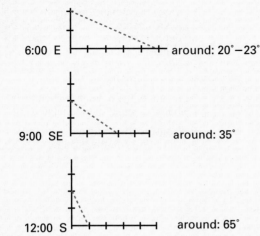

6:00 E around: 20°–23°

9:00 SE around: 35°

12:00 S around: 65°

5.

Time of Day	Direction of Sun	Length of Shadow	Angle of Sun's Ray
6:00 A.M.	E	5 m	around 20°–23°
9:00 A.M.	SE	around 3 m	around 35°
12:00 P.M.	S	around 1 m	around 65°
3:00 P.M.	SW	around 3 m	around 35°
6:00 P.M.	W	around 5 m	around 20°–23°

Hints and Comments

Materials

straightedges or rulers (one per student); protractors or compass cards (one per student)

Overview

Students create a table containing information about the direction of the sun, the length of a shadow, and the angle of the sun's rays at different times of the day.

About the Mathematics

Students investigate how the lengths of shadows and the angles of the sun's rays vary in the course of a day. The appropriate representation of the context is a side-view scale drawing. The underlying mathematical structure of the situation is that of a right triangle: The light ray is the hypotenuse, the vertical object causing the shadow is the height, and the shadow is the base. Students draw only one sun's ray hitting the tree and measure the angle it makes with the ground. Of course there are numerous sun's rays near the tree, but at one particular moment of the day all these rays are equally steep and have the same angle with the ground.

Planning

Students may work on problems 4–5 in small groups. You may want to discuss the completed table with the whole class.

B **Shadows and Blind Spots**

Notes

6 Before completing this problem talk about the distance being half the height of the building. Give examples: If the building is 15 m, the shadow would be 7.5 m. Hint to get started: measure the building.

7 When drawing these right triangles, the larger the drawing, the more precise the angle measurement will be.

7a and 8a Have students share drawings on the overhead.

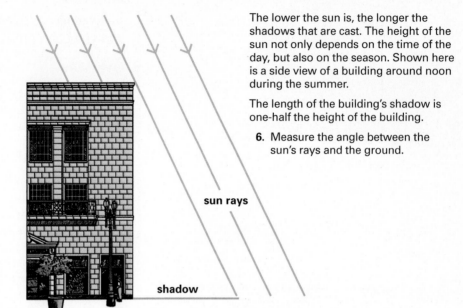

The lower the sun is, the longer the shadows that are cast. The height of the sun not only depends on the time of the day, but also on the season. Shown here is a side view of a building around noon during the summer.

The length of the building's shadow is one-half the height of the building.

6. Measure the angle between the sun's rays and the ground.

sun rays

shadow

Around noon during the winter, the length of this building's shadow is two times the height of the building.

7. a. Draw a side view of the building and its shadow around noon during the winter.

 b. Measure the angle between the sun's rays and the ground.

Around noon during the spring, the angle between the sun's rays and the ground is 45°.

8. a. Draw a side view of the building and its shadow around noon during the spring.

 b. If the building is 40 m tall, how long is its shadow?

9. Describe the changes in the length of the shadow and the angle of the sun's rays from season to season.

Assessment Pyramid

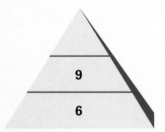

Understand the ratio between the lengths of an object and its shadow caused by the sun.
Measure angles.

Reaching All Learners

Intervention

To help students complete the problems on this page, have students begin a table with the following column headings:

Season	Building Height	Shadow Length	Ratio of Shadow:Building	Angle

Advanced Learners

Ask, *Why is there a change in shadow length with the change of seasons?* (In the Northern Hemisphere, the sun is lower in the sky throughout the day in the winter and higher in the sky in the summer.)

Solutions and Samples

6. The angle is about 63°.

7. a.

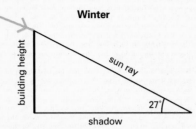

Winter

building height

sun ray

shadow

27°

b. The angle is 27°.

8. a.

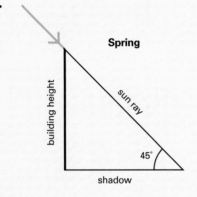

Spring

building height

sun ray

shadow

45°

b. The length of the shadow is equal to the height of the building, which is 40 meters.

9. Descriptions will vary. Students may make a table using all the information they have gathered, as shown below.

Season	Angle of Sun's Rays	Building Height	Length of Shadow
Summer	63	40 m	20 m
Winter	27	40 m	80 m
Spring	45	40 m	40 m

At noon on a summer's day, the sun can appear to be almost directly overhead, and shadows are very short. In the fall, the shadows gradually get longer and the angle of the sun's rays gradually gets smaller. In the winter, the noontime sun is relatively low and creates long shadows. In the spring, the angle of the sun's rays increases gradually, and shadows get shorter.

Hints and Comments

Materials

straightedges or rulers (one per student); protractors and/or compass cards (one per student); graph paper, optional (several sheets per student)

Overview

Students reflect on how the lengths of shadows and the angles of the sun's rays vary depending on the season. Students make side-view drawings of a building, its shadow, and the sun's rays for three seasons. These drawings are right triangles.

Planning

Students may work on problems 6–9 in small groups. You may want to discuss these problems with the whole class.

Comments About the Solutions

6. Students should measure the angle with a protractor or compass card.

7. Students' drawings may use different scales. In any case, the length of the shadow should be two times the height of the building. You may ask students why drawings using different scales give the same angle measurement.

8. Again, students' drawings may use different scales. Students should discover that with a 45° angle, the ratio between the height of the building and the length of the shadow is 1:1.

Shadows and Blind Spots

Notes

Students could work on this as a group, setting up a few per class, and having each class measure the shadow during their class time.

Provide a one meter string for each student to measure the lengths they need since many will not have a meter stick at home. If students do not have a compass at home, they can leave that column blank.

Activity

In this activity, you will investigate the shadows caused by the sun. On a sunny day, you will measure the shadow and the angle of the sun's rays.

First, you need to assemble your angle measuring tool (AMT). Cut out the figure on **Student Activity Sheet 4** along the solid lines. Make the first fold as shown here and glue the matching shaded pieces together. Continue to fold your AMT in the order shown.

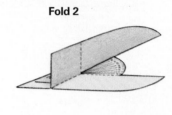

Fold 1　　　　　　　**Fold 2**

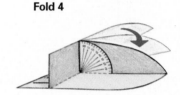

Fold 3　　　　　　　**Fold 4**

You will need the following items:

- a stick about 1.2 m long
- a stick about 0.7 m long
- a metric tape measure
- several meters of string
- your AMT
- a directional compass

Reaching All Learners

Parental Involvement

This activity could be assigned as a family project for extra credit.

Hints and Comments

Materials

Student Activity Sheet 4 (one per student);
scissors (one pair per student);
glue (one bottle per pair of students);
cardstock, optional (one sheet per student)

Overview

Students build an angle measurement tool. They will use it to investigate the shadows caused by the sun. There are no problems on this page for students to solve.

About the Mathematics

The underlying mathematical structure of the situation is again that of a right triangle. The light ray is the hypotenuse, the vertical object causing the shadow is the height, and the shadow is the base.

Planning

Copy **Student Activity Sheet 4** onto cardstock, which is sturdier than regular paper and will make a more accurate angle measurement tool.

Shadows and
Blind Spots

Notes

Some students may not know how to use a directional compass. The compass should be held flat, with the needle lined up with the mark for North. The compass can then be laid in the path of the shadow to mark the direction of the sun.

Drive both sticks into the ground about 2 m apart. The longer stick should have a height of 1 m above the ground, and the shorter stick should have a height of 0.5 m above the ground. The sticks should be perfectly vertical.

In your notebook, copy the following table. Take measurements at least five different times during the day and fill in your table. Add more blank rows to your table as needed.

		0.5-meter Stick		1-meter Stick	
Time of Day	Direction of Sun	Length of Shadow (in cm)	Angle of Sun's Rays	Length of Shadow (in cm)	Angle of Sun's Rays

Use the compass to determine the direction from which the sun is shining. Use the tape measure to measure the lengths of the shadows of both sticks, and use your AMT and string (as shown below) to measure the angle between the sun's rays and the ground for both sticks. Be sure to stretch the string to where the shadow ends and place your AMT there.

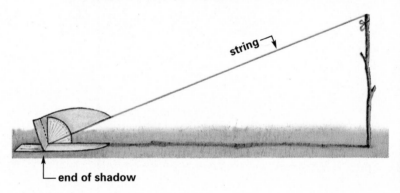

string

└─ end of shadow

Reaching All Learners

Accommodation

This activity is designed to be completed when the sun is shining. If it is impossible to do this experiment outside, either at school or at home, it can be replaced by an indoor simulation using a strong light. However, you will not be able to model the sun exactly.

Solutions and Samples

Answers will vary, depending on the number of measurements taken, the time of day, the season, the location, and so on. Sample measurements:

Time of Day	Direction of Sun	0.5-meter Stick		1-meter Stick	
		Length of Shadow (in cm)	Angle of Sun's Rays	Length of Shadow (in cm)	Angle of Sun's Rays
11 A.M.	Southeast	50 cm	45°	100 cm	45°
4 P.M.	Southwest	100 cm	27°	200 cm	27°

Hints and Comments

Materials

string (one roll per pair of students);
scissors (one pair per student);
directional compasses (one per student);
metric measuring tapes (one per student);
sticks, 0.7 meter long (one per student);
sticks, 1.2 meters long (one per student);
angle measurement tools constructed by students on the previous page (one per student)

Planning

Students may do the Activity individually or in small groups. It may also be assigned as homework over a weekend. Alternatively, you might plan with other teachers to have students take measures for one full day.

Comments About the Activity

This activity may be assigned as homework.

Students should use the sticks to create shadows. They should put the sticks in the ground in an open area to avoid interfering shadows from surrounding objects. Students should use the string to model the sun's rays. To measure the angle of the sun's rays, students should place the angle measurement tool flat on the ground. The vertical flap should align perfectly with the string.

The earlier in the day students start measuring, the lower the sun will be, the smaller the angle, and the longer the shadows. In other words, you will get a greater range of measures. Be sure to have students note the date and season that the measures were taken, as well as the location.

Shadows and Blind Spots

Notes

Do this page as a class discussion and develop four summary statements that focus on problems 10b, 10c, 11a, 12a, and 12b.

11a Set up a ratio of the shadow length:height of stick.

11b Have students define *parallel*. (Parallel lines are equidistant apart and therefore never intersect.)

Use your data from the table you made in the activity on pages 16 and 17 to answer the following problems.

10. a. Describe the movement of the sun during the day.

   b. Describe how the direction of the shadow changes throughout the day. How are the shadows related to the direction from which the sun is shining?

   c. Describe the changes in the length of the shadow throughout the day. When are the shadows longest and when are they shortest?

Compare the shadows of the longer stick with the shadows of the shorter stick.

11. a. Describe the relationship between the length of the shadow and the height of the stick.

   b. Were the shadows of the two sticks parallel at all times? Explain.

Compare the angle of the sun's rays for each stick at any moment during the day.

12. a. Describe how the angle of the sun's rays changed during the day. When is the angle the greatest, and when is it the smallest?

   b. How is the size of the angle of the sun's rays related to the length of the shadows?

Shadows Cast by the Sun and Lights

The sun causes parallel objects to cast parallel shadows. In this photograph, for example, the bars of the railing cast parallel shadows on the sidewalk.

Assessment Pyramid

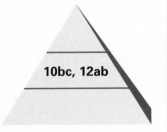

10bc, 12ab

Understand the ratio between an object and its shadow and the relationship between angles and the height-to-distance ratio.

Reaching All Learners

Extension

Challenge students with the following questions:

• *How would the size of the angles of the sun be different during another season?* (Summer days are longer than winter days. Also the sun is higher in the summer. The angle of the sun's rays and the length of the shadow change accordingly.)

• *How would the size of the angle of the sun be different if you lived closer to the Equator?* (The sun is higher when you are closer to the Equator, so shadows are shorter and the angle of the sun's rays is larger.)

• *How would your measurements be different if you lived in the Southern Hemisphere?* (The sun travels across the northern part of the sky.)

Solutions and Samples

10. a. Descriptions will vary. Sample response:

   The sun rises in the east and sets in the west. Also, in the Northern Hemisphere, the sun travels across the southern part of the sky.

b. Descriptions will vary. Sample response:

   The direction of the shadows is exactly opposite the direction from which the sun is shining (a difference of 180°).

c. Descriptions will vary. Sample response:

   The shadows are longest at the beginning and end of the day. They are shortest at noon.

11. a. Descriptions will vary. Sample response:

   The shadow of the shorter stick is always half the length of the longer stick; provided you measure the shadows at the same time. So, at any given moment of the day, the ratio between an object's length and that of its shadow is constant.

b. Yes. Explanations will vary. Sample explanations:

   If the sticks are vertical, the shadows will always be parallel because the sun's rays are all parallel.

   The sun hits the sticks at the same angle.

12. a. When the sun is near the horizon, the angles are small. This happens near sunrise and sunset.

   At noon, the angles are larger.

b. When the sun is low in the sky, the angle of the sun's ray is small, causing long shadows. When the sun is high in the sky, the angle of the sun's ray is large which makes shorter shadows.

Hints and Comments

Overview

Students analyze the data they collected in the previous Activity and draw conclusions.

About the Mathematics

The ratios between the heights and shadow lengths of objects are the same when measured at the same time of the day. However, the height-to-shadow length ratio varies for different times of the day.

Planning

Students may work on problems 10–12 individually. These problems may also be assigned as homework.

Comments About the Problems

12. b. Students may give their answers in words, or they may make a graph with times of day on the *x*-axis and the lengths of the shadows on the *y*-axis.

Writing Opportunity

You may want to have students write a report explaining their data and the results of the activity. Students should include data, drawings, tables, and graphs in their reports.

B Shadows and Blind Spots

Notes

13 Before answering this problem you may want students to investigate shadows caused by a lamp. For this purpose you may use a stationary, high-powered lamp (overhead projector) and objects of different heights placed at different distances from the lamp.

13 Be sure students have a clear understanding of the solution for this problem before advancing to problem 14.

A streetlight causes a completely different picture.

13. Explain the differences between the shadows caused by the streetlight and the shadows caused by the sun and the reasons for these differences.

This is a picture of a streetlight surrounded by posts.

14. On **Student Activity Sheet 5**, draw in the missing shadows. It is nighttime in top view A, so the streetlight is shining. It is daytime in top view B, so the streetlight is off, and the sun is shining.

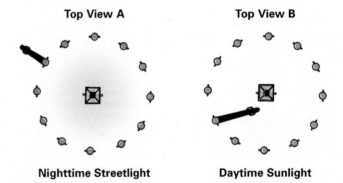

Top View A   **Top View B**

Nighttime Streetlight   **Daytime Sunlight**

Assessment Pyramid

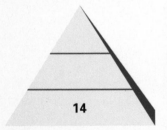

14

Construct light rays and shadows in two-dimensional representations.

Reaching All Learners

Act It Out

Have students hold pencils up and show where the shadow would be in relation to the sun's location. They should notice that all the shadows are parallel. Select a student to be a lamp. Have students indicate the shadows cast from the lamp. They should notice that the shadows fan out from the light source.

Solutions and Samples

13. Answers will vary. Sample response:

The sun is very far away from us. The sun's rays are parallel. Therefore parallel objects, like the bars of the railing in the photograph on page 18, cause parallel shadows.

A lamp is much closer to the objects. The light comes from one point and therefore the light rays spread out in an array, and as a consequence so do the shadows (as shown in the photograph on top of page 19).

14. Top View A

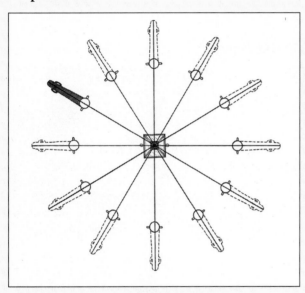

Top View B

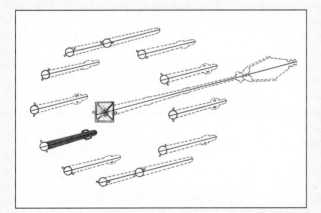

Hints and Comments

Materials

Student Activity Sheet 5
A stationary, high-powered lamp (overhead projector), optional;
objects of different heights, optional

Overview

Students describe the differences between the shadows caused by a nearby light source and shadows caused by the sun. Students also use what they learned about differences between shadows caused by a light and shadows caused by the sun in order to draw shadows caused by sunlight and by a streetlight.

About the Mathematics

Shadows caused by the sun are different from shadows caused by a nearby light source. Both the direction and the lengths of the shadows are different. Shadows caused by the sun do not fan out but are parallel, and the lengths of the shadows depend on the height of the sun and the time of year.

Planning

Students may work on problem 13 in small groups. Discuss student answers in class. Students may work on problem 14 individually.

Comments About the Solutions

14. In the first picture, all shadows should be equally long, and they should be fanning out from the lamp. In the second picture, all shadows of the posts are also equally long, but they should be parallel to each other. To make their drawings complete, students should also include the shadow of the streetlight. To estimate the length of the streetlight's shadow, students should remember that at a given time of the day, the ratio between an object's length and the length of its shadow is constant.

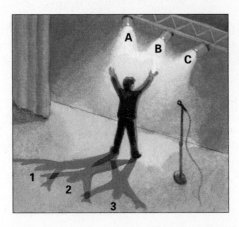

This is a picture of a singer on stage. Three different spotlights are used in the performance. Three shadows are formed on the stage.

15. Which light creates which shadow?

A Shadow Is a Blind Spot

Here are two boats.

One picture shows the blind spot of the captain on the boat during the day. The other picture shows the shadow of the boat at nighttime, caused by a searchlight.

16. Explain why these pictures are almost exactly the same.

16 Students should understand the relationship between blind spots and shadows and be able to connect Section A and B. What the eye does not see, a light would not reach either.

Reaching All Learners

Extension

Have students investigate their shadow patterns when there are multiple light sources in a room. With two or more overhead projectors or strong flashlights in a darkened room, students could observe the multiple shadows cast by their pencils.

Solutions and Samples

15. Light A creates shadow 3.

Light B creates shadow 2.

Light C creates shadow 1.

16. Answers may vary. Sample response:

The pictures are the same because vision lines for the captain act very much like the light rays for the search light. What the captain cannot see, the light cannot touch.

The vision lines "produce" a blind area or blind spot.

The light rays "produce" a shadow.

The shadow and blind area look identical (the same).

Hints and Comments

Overview

Students relate a shadow to the light source creating it. They also reflect on the similarity between a shadow and a blind spot.

Planning

Students may work on problem 15 individually. Problem 16 may be done in small groups. Discuss students' answers to problem 16 in class.

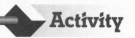

Shadows and Blind Spots

Notes

Use connecting cubes or blocks for this activity.

Make sure students are able to draw vision lines correctly. If not, you might have students look carefully at their tugboats from the viewpoints indicated on Student Activity Sheet 6. While one student watches, his or her partner could identify the captain's vision line with string, a straw, or a piece of uncooked spaghetti.

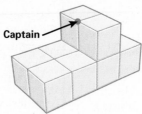

Captain

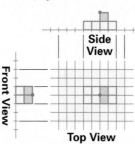

Side View

Front View

Top View

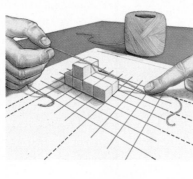

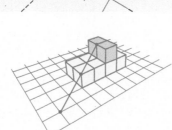

In this activity, you will investigate the blind area of a tugboat.

- Use 1-cm blocks to build a model of the tugboat.

- Place your boat on the top-view outline on **Student Activity Sheet 6**.

- Use string to represent the captain's vision line.

On **Student Activity Sheet 6**, draw the captain's vision lines for the side, top, and front views.

In the top view, shade the area of the graph paper that represents the blind area of the boat.

On **Student Activity Sheet 7**, draw vision lines and shade the blind area for the view shown. One vision line has already been drawn.

Reaching All Learners

Intervention

Have students look at their boats from eye level in order to see the vision lines. Turn the boat to face the necessary view.

Extension

You may want to redesign the cube boat (or move the captain's bridge) and have students delineate the blind area of the new boat.

Solutions and Samples

Student Activity Sheet 6:

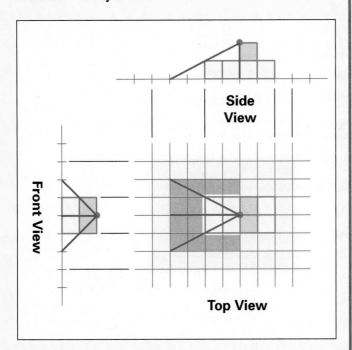

Side View

Front View

Top View

Student Activity Sheet 7:

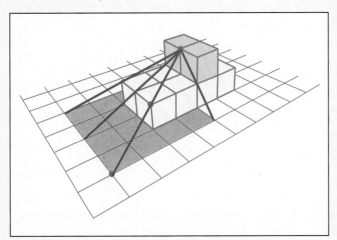

Hints and Comments

Materials

Student Activity Sheets 6 and 7 (one per student); pieces of string, straws, or uncooked spaghetti (one per pair of students); centimeter cubes (at least 10 per pair of students)

Overview

Students build a model of a tugboat and find the blind area for the tugboat's captain.

About the Mathematics

This activity focuses students' attention on the exact construction of a blind area and its shape. It forms a bridge between the canyon tables activity from Section A—where the marks on the opposite wall were all on the same level—and this section, where students find that the shadow of a straight object will form a straight shadow. The shape of a shadow is similar to the shape of the object casting the shadow, just like the shape of the blind area of a boat is similar to the boat itself.

Planning

Students may work on the activity in pairs.

Comments About the Solutions

Discuss the kind of information that is captured and lost in **Student Activity Sheet 6**'s point of view. In the side view, students see where the vision lines hit the water in front. In the front view, they see where the vision lines hit the water at the sides. In the top view, they see the directions of the vision lines.

The drawing on **Student Activity Sheet 7** builds on what students did on **Student Activity Sheet 6**. Students should be able to use the information they gathered earlier in this activity to shade in the blind area.

B Shadows and Blind Spots

Summary ⟫

Shadows can be caused by two kinds of light:

- light that is nearby, such as a streetlight;
- light that is very far away, such as the sun.

When the light comes from the sun, the rays of light are parallel, and the shadows of parallel lines are parallel.

When the light comes from a lamp, the shadows are cast in different directions. They resemble vision lines.

For that reason, shadows are similar to blind spots or blind areas.

As the sun moves, shadows will too.

A sun low in the sky casts long shadows.

A sun high in the sky casts short shadows.

The shadows caused by the sun do not only change in length, they also change in direction. In the morning shadows will stretch toward the west.

Check Your Work ⟫

The model of a tugboat has a searchlight at point A.

In order to show the shadow caused by the searchlight, two rays of light are drawn.

1. Use **Student Activity Sheet 8** to draw and shade in the shadow of the tugboat caused by the searchlight.

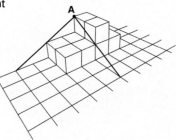

1 Be sure students notice the location of the searchlight since it is different from the captain's location on the previous page.

Assessment Pyramid

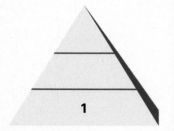

Assesses Section B Goals

Reaching All Learners

English Language Learners

With a partner, create a drawing for each point made in the Summary.

Accommodation

Have cubes available for problem 1 and refer students to their drawings for **Student Activity Sheets 6** and **7**.

Solutions and Samples

Answers to Check Your Work

1.

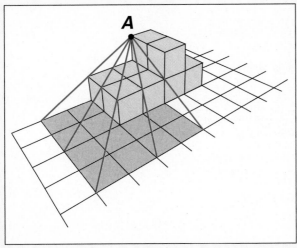

Materials

Student Activity Sheet 8 (one per student)

Overview

Students read the Summary, which reviews the main concepts covered in this section. Students use the Check Your Work problems as self-assessment. The answers to these problems are also provided on pages 62 and 63 of the Student Book. After students complete Section A, you may assign as homework appropriate activities from the Additional Practice section, located on page 57 of the Student Book. After students complete Sections A and B, you may use Quiz 1 with students as a mid-unit assessment.

Planning

Problem 1 may be used for students' self-assessment.

Solutions and Samples

11.

Steepness Table					
α (angle measure in degrees)	**27°**	**30°**	**45°**	**60°**	**63°**
h:d (ratio of height to distance)	1:2 = 0.5	4:7 = 0.57	1:1 = 1.0	7:4 = 1.75	2:1 = 2.0

12.

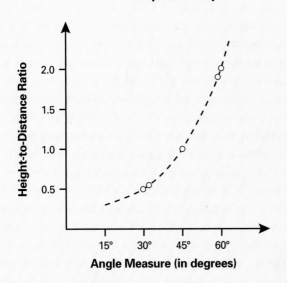

Steepness Graph

13. The larger the angle, the larger the ratio of height to distance. The ratio increases faster than the angle increases.

14. To be safe, the ladder can be positioned at any angle between 64° and 71°.

Hints and Comments

Materials

centimeter rulers (one per student);
ladder, optional (one per class);
graph paper (two sheets per student)

Overview

Students make a table and a graph of steepness and angles of elevation. They describe the relationship between the two. They also investigate the height-to-distance ratios at which a ladder can be positioned safely.

About the Mathematics

The table students fill in for problem 11 will be used again in Section D, where students investigate a table of the tangent in the context of glide ratios.

Planning

Students may work on problems 11–13 individually. Problems 11 and 12 may also be assigned as homework. Be sure to discuss problem 13 in class. Students may continue working on problem 14 in small groups.

Comments About the Solutions

11. This problem is critical because it focuses students' attention on the relationship between steepness and angle of elevation. Make sure students have the correct data from problem 10. The ratio $h:d$ may be expressed as a fraction or a decimal.

12. Again, students need the correct answers from problem 10. The height-to-distance ratio should now be expressed as a decimal because this makes it easier to label the axes.

14. A height-to-distance ratio between two and three is safe for most ladders, but it depends on the ladder.

Shadows and Angles

Notes

For the Summary, be sure to review how to change the height:distance ratio to a decimal. Example 3:5 = 0.6.

Have students use graph paper for Check Your Work.

1 If students struggle with this problem, refer them to problem 10, page 28.

Summary

As the angle between a ladder and the ground increases, the height of the position of the ladder on the wall increases. At the same time, the distance between the foot of the ladder and the wall decreases.

In the same way, as the angle between a ray of sunlight and the ground increases, a shadow on the ground becomes shorter.

The steepness of a ladder can be measured in the following two ways:

- by the angle (the greater the angle, the steeper the ladder);
- by the ratio of height to distance, or *h:d* (the greater the ratio, the steeper the ladder).

Check Your Work

1. Use a compass card or a protractor and a ruler to make scale drawings of a ladder leaning against a wall for each of the following situations:

   a. $\alpha = 60°$

   b. $h = 3, d = 1$

   c. Measure and record α from problem **b.**

Assessment Pyramid

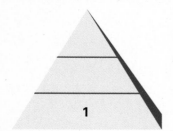

Assesses Section C Goals

Reaching All Learners

Intervention

Students may need help setting up these problems.

(For example: for problem 1a, students should initially draw a horizontal line which represents the floor, then a vertical line somewhere at the right side of the floor, which represents the wall. Then they choose a point on the floor at a certain distance from the wall. At that point, they should measure a 60° angle to draw the ladder. They may have to extend the height of the wall.)

Solutions and Samples

Answers to Check Your Work

1. a.

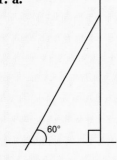

b.

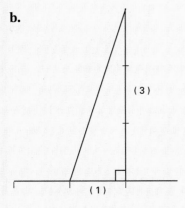

c. $\alpha \approx 72°$.

Hints and Comments

Materials

compass card or protractor (one per student); rulers (one per student)

Overview

Students read the Summary, which reviews the main concepts covered in this section. Students use the Check Your Work problems as self-assessment. The answers to these problems are also provided on Student Book page 64. After students complete Section C, you may assign as homework appropriate activities from the Additional Practice section, located on Student Book page 58.

Planning

Problem 1 may be used for students' self-assessment.

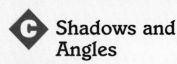
2 Specify to students that they should use centimeters.

3 Have students draw triangles formed from the vision lines. Label height and distance in order to compare the two triangles.

For Further Reflection

Reflective questions are meant to summarize and discuss important concepts.

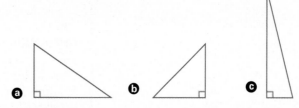

Here are three different scale drawings of right triangles, each representing a "ladder situation."

2. For each ladder situation, use the scale drawing to find α, *h, d,* and *h:d*.

Here is a drawing of a cross-section of another canyon model, like the one you worked with in Section A. The numbers indicate the scale of the height and the width of the ledges and the width of the river.

3. Which vision line is steeper, the one from point A down to the river or the one from point B down to the river? Support your answer with information about the angle between the vision line and the river and the ratio of the height to the distance.

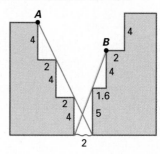

For Further Reflection

Explain how you could use shadows to estimate the height of a tower.

Assessment Pyramid

☐FFR

3

2

Assesses Section C Goals

Reaching All Learners

Advanced Learners

Choose another ledge for the height and find the height-to-distance ratio. What do you notice?

Intervention

As students complete the For Further Reflection problem, you may need to remind students of their findings in the shadow measuring activity on pages 16 and 17 and in particular of their conclusion for problem 11a. Encourage students to give an example involving numbers.

Solutions and Samples

2.

	α	h	d	$\frac{h}{d}$
a.	34°	2	3	$\frac{2}{3}$
b.	45°	2	2	1
c.	76°	4	1	4

3. Vision line from ledge B is steeper.

Explanations may vary. Here are two.

Using the canyon scale information, I constructed a right triangle for each situation and found α. It is larger toward ledge B, making it steeper.

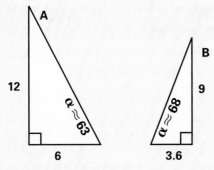

I compared *h:d* for both: 12:6 and 9:3.6. This is like 2:1 compared to 2.5:1. Since this 2.5:1 is larger, the line to goes up faster and is steeper.

For Further Reflection

Answers will vary. Sample response:

If you want to find out how high a building is without actually measuring it on a sunny day, you can use its shadow. First you measure the length of the building's shadow. Suppose it's 80 meters long. Then you put a 1-meter stick upright on the ground and measure its shadow. Suppose the shadow of the stick is 2 meters long. This means that the shadow at that time of the day is twice as long as the height of the object casting the shadow. In the case of the building, this implies that the height of the building is half of the length of the shadow, which is 40 meters. In a ratio table:

height object	1	40
length shadow	2	80

Hints and Comments

Materials

compass cards or protractors (one per student); centimeter rulers (one per student)

Planning

Problems 2–3 may be used for student self-assessment.

Comments About the Solutions

2. You may encourage students to record the data of the three triangles in a table.

3. This problem makes a connection with Section A, where students investigated vision lines in the context of the Grand Canyon. You may refer to the activity with the table canyon on Student Book page 3. The vision line of a taller person (or a person sitting nearer the edge of the canyon wall) was steeper; therefore this person could see more of the river.

Students can determine the steeper vision line by comparing the ratios of the two vision lines, concluding which ratio is bigger, and deducing which angle must be larger. Students might also compare the sizes of the angles and deduce which height-to-distance ratio must be bigger. Either approach is fine, as long as students use the data of ratio and angle to support their answers.

You may want to discuss the advantages and disadvantages of using ratios instead of protractors to find angles.

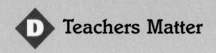 Teachers Matter

Section Focus

The instructional focus of Section D is to:

- make side-view drawings (to scale) of the glide path of different gliders;
- compare the performance of different gliders using the glide ratio;
- make a steepness table and find equivalent glide ratios, fractions, and decimals;
- describe the relationship between the glide ratio, glide angle, and tangent;
- use formal tangent notation and use tangent to solve problems; and
- use a tangent table or the tangent key on a scientific calculator.

Pacing and Planning

Day 12: Hang Gliders		Student pages 32–35
INTRODUCTION	Problems 1 and 2	Explore the ratio of height of take-off to the distance traveled.
CLASSWORK	Problems 3–6	Use a ratio table and the glide ratio to determine the height of take-off or the distance traveled for different hang glider flights.
HOMEWORK	Problems 7 and 8	Create scale drawings of glide ratios.

Day 13: Hang Gliders (Continued)		Student pages 36 and 37
INTRODUCTION	Review homework.	Review homework from Day 12.
CLASSWORK	Problems 9–12	Determine the glide angle that corresponds to each glide ratio.
HOMEWORK	Problem 13	Compare different glide ratios and graph the relationship between glide angles and ratios.

Day 14: From Glide Ratio to Tangent (Continued)		Student pages 38 and 39
INTRODUCTION	Problems 14 and 15	Introduce the relationship between the glide ratio and the tangent and calculate the tangent.
CLASSWORK	Problems 16–18	Make scale drawings of right triangles to find angle measures and side lengths.
HOMEWORK	Problem 19	Use the tangent of an angle to solve a problem involving a ladder leaning against a wall.

Day 15: From Glide Ratio to Tangent (Continued)		Student pages 40–44
INTRODUCTION	Review homework. Problems 20–22	Review homework from Day 14 and explore the relationship between the tangent ratio and angle measures.
CLASSWORK	Problem 23 Check Your Work	Student self-assessment: Use the tangent ratio to solve right triangle problems.
HOMEWORK	For Further Reflection	Explain the mathematical relationship between different problem contexts.

Day 16: Summary		
INTRODUCTION	Review	Review problems from Day 15.
ASSESSMENT	Quiz 2	Assessment of Section C and D Goals.

Additional Resources: Additional Practice, Section D, Student Book pages 58 and 59

Materials

Student Resources

Quantities listed are per student.

- **Student Activity Sheet 11**
  - Appendix A on Teacher's Guide pages 61A–62 (Student Book pages 68–70)

Teachers Resources

No resources required

Student Materials

Quantities listed are per student.

- Centimeter rulers
- Protractors or compass cards

* See Hints and Comments for optional materials.

Learning Lines

Formalization of Steepness as the Tangent Ratio

The mathematical content of this section is introduced in the context of hang gliders. It naturally motivates a strategy to compare the performance of different gliders. Two different measures may be used: the size of the glide angle (the angle between the flight path and the ground) or the glide ratio (the ratio between the height the glider is launched from and the distance it covers as measured on the ground).

Represented in a side view, the situation is very similar to that of a ladder.

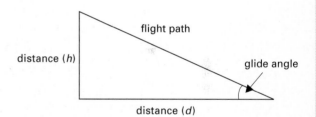

The previous sections have been preparing students for this formal introduction of the tangent. It is important at this point that students learn how to use the appropriate mathematical language (such as: the ratio $h{:}d$ is also called the *tangent of angle* α), formal notation (for example: $\tan 35° = \frac{7}{10} = 0.7$), and mathematical tools (tangent table, calculator).

At the End of This Section: Learning Outcomes

Students understand that the glide ratio is the tangent of the glide angle. They can express the glide ratio in fractions and decimals. Students understand the relationship between the size of an angle and its tangent value. Students can use formal tangent notation and apply their understanding of tangent in solving problems.

Glide Angles

Notes

Ask students to share their knowledge of gliders (and paper airplanes!). What are the differences in the design between a glider and a passenger airplane?

Hang Gliders

Hang gliders are light, kite-like gliders that carry a pilot in a harness. The pilot takes off from a hill or a cliff into the wind. The hang glider then slowly descends to the ground.

When pilots make their first flight with a new glider, they are very careful because they do not know how quickly the glider will descend.

Reaching All Learners

Act It Out

In order to peak students' interest in the new context, have students make paper airplanes and have a contest to find out whose plane flies the farthest. Do taller people have an advantage?

Materials

model glider airplane, optional (one per class)

Overview

Students begin this section by reading about hang gliders. There are no problems on this page for students to solve.

About the Mathematics

The context of the hang glider is similar to the other three contexts featured in the previous sections. All contexts involve steepness and can be represented with a right triangle: the steepness of the vision line in the context of the canyon, the steepness of the vision line of the captain on a ship, the steepness of ladders, and, in this section, the steepness of the flight path of the hang glider.

Students investigate the glide ratio: a general ratio in which the steepness of the path varies and the height is fixed at 1. The steeper path will have a large glide ratio such as 1:1 or 1:0.5, with a value larger than 1. A less steep path would have a glide ratio of 1:2 or 1:20, with a value less than 1. The glide angle is also investigated. The glide angle (as shown in the figure below) is the angle the flight path makes with the ground. A steeper path has a glide angle of between 45 and 90 degrees. A less steep path has a glide angle of between 0 and 45 degrees. In reality, the safest glide angle for a hang glider is about 6 degrees or smaller.

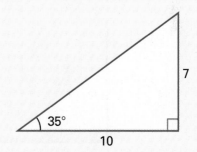

The right triangles of hang gliding are used to study the tangent function of the angle of any right triangle. The ratio of height to distance is equal to the tangent of the angle opposite the height.

In the example shown here, the tangent of the 35° angle is 0.7. By looking at a table of tangent values for angles ranging from 0 to 90 degrees (see Appendix A on Teacher's Guide pages 61A–62), it can be seen that the tangent ratio increases slowly for the first 45 degrees, ranging from 0 to 1, and then increases rapidly as the angle increases from 45 to 90 degrees. The section ends with students solving problems using the tangent relationship.

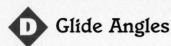
Notes

1 and 2 Use a ratio table. Do 1 as a class discussion.

2 Remind students that the distance is from the ground to the cliff, not the path of the glider.

3 Students should use graph paper and draw triangles to scale.

Marianne, the pilot in this picture, decides to make her first jump from a 10-m cliff. She glides along a straight line, covering 40 m of ground as shown in the drawing.

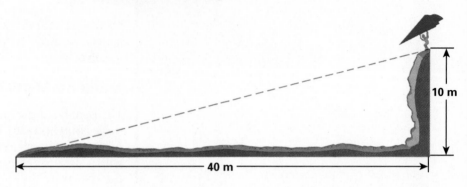

After several successful flights, she decides to go to a higher cliff. This cliff is 15 m high.

1. How much ground distance does the glider cover from the higher cliff? Note: Assume that the steepness of the flight path remains the same.

2. Marianne makes flights from three cliffs that are 20 m, 50 m, and 100 m high. How much ground distance does the glider cover on each flight?

Marianne has designed a glider that can travel farther than her first one. With the new glider, Marianne claims, "When I jump from a 10-m cliff, I can cover 70 m of ground!"

3. **a.** Draw a side view of Marianne's flight path with the new glider.

   b. Copy the table below and complete it for the new glider.

Height (in m)	10	25	100			
Distance (in m)	70			245		1,000

Reaching All Learners

Accommodation

How high is a 10 m cliff? Show a meter stick and talk about a meter being close to three feet. (30 yards on a football field)

Intervention

Review ratio tables with various operations (doubling, halving, adding columns etc.) If students have difficulty, you might also have them sketch side views of the flight paths.

Solutions and Samples

1. The glider covers 60 meters. Students may use a drawing. Others might use a ratio table:

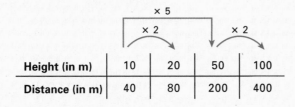

	÷ 2		× 3
Height (in m)	10	5	15
Distance (in m)	40	20	60

2. Answer are recorded in the table:

Height (in m)	20	50	100
Distance (in m)	80	200	400

Here's a ratio table solution:

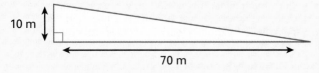

	× 2	× 5	× 2
Height (in m)	10	20	50	100
Distance (in m)	40	80	200	400

3. a. The size of the triangle may vary depending on the scale that is used. Sample solution:

10 m

70 m

b.

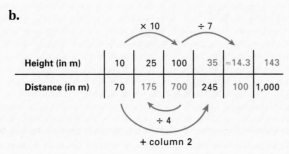

	× 10	÷ 7			
Height (in m)	10	25	100	35	≈14.3	143
Distance (in m)	70	175	700	245	100	1,000

÷ 4

+ column 2

Hints and Comments

Materials

centimeter rulers (one per student)

Overview

Students use ratio tables to find out how far a glider will fly from various heights when the distance for one height is given.

About the Mathematics

At the start of the section, students look at a glider with a fixed height-to-distance ratio, so the steepness of its flight path is constant. Side-view drawings of different flights of this glider will look like similar triangles; the angle between the flight path and the ground remains the same.

Next, students investigate gliders with a different height-to-distance ratio. Further on in the section, students need to develop a measure (the "glide ratio") in order to compare the performances of different hang gliders.

Planning

You may want to have students work on problem 1 as a whole-class activity. They may work on problems 2 and 3 in small groups. Discuss students' answers.

Comments About the Solutions

1.–3. For these problems, distance refers to the distance covered on the ground. So when a problem asks how far the glider flew, the solution is not the length of the flight path of the glider (the hypotenuse of the right triangle formed by height, distance, and flight path). The distance is the ground distance covered by the glider.

3. a. Tell students to sketch a side view that is drawn to scale. You might have students determine an appropriate scale themselves. For example, 1 centimeter could represent 10 meters.

D Glide Angles

Notes

4 Clarify that students should trace the path of the glider and use this to create a right triangle.

4c Note that this refers to problems 1 and 3.

5 Discuss this problem to be sure students understand glide ratio.

2 cm

16.3 cm

This picture is based on three separate photographs, taken one after the other. It shows a model glider that is used in laboratory experiments. By taking three pictures within a short period of time, you can determine the path of the glider.

4. In your notebook, trace the path of this glider and make a scale drawing similar to the drawing on top of page 33. Use your scale drawing to answer the following questions.

   a. If the glider in the picture is launched from a height of 5 m, how far will the glider fly before landing?

   b. How far will the glider fly from a 10-m cliff?

   c. Compare the distances covered by Marianne's two hang gliders and this model glider. If all three are launched from 10 m, which one flies the farthest? Explain.

Glide Ratio

To determine which hang glider travels farther, you can consider the **glide ratio**. Marianne's first glider flew 40 m from a 10-m cliff. This glider has a glide ratio of 1:4 (one to four). Marianne's second glider flew 70 m from a 10-m cliff.

The second glider has a glide ratio of 1:7.

5. What do you think a glide ratio is?

Assessment Pyramid

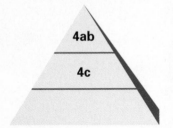

4ab

4c

Use ratios to solve problems and make relative comparisons involving steepness problems.

Reaching All Learners

Extension

Review ways to write ratios: $\frac{1}{3}$, 1:3, 1 to 3.

Vocabulary Building

A *glide ratio* is height:distance. Have students draw a picture of a glider and its path and label it with the height, distance, and α angle.

Solutions and Samples

4. a. About 41 meters. Answers may vary somewhat due to measurement errors. Strategies will vary. Sample strategies:

- The ratio is 2:16.3, which is about 1:8.2. Launched from a height of 5 meters, the glider will travel about 41 meters.

- Using a ratio table, I used my drawing measurements, but changed them to meters since I need to get to a height of 5 m.

Height (in m)	2	1	5
Distance (in m)	16.3	8.2	41

b. 82 m.

In problem a. I found that launched from a height of 1 meter, the plane will get about 8.2 meters far. So from a height of 10 meters, this will be 82 meters.

c. The model glider flies the farthest.

I put the information in one chart, making the height all the same (10 m).

Height	Distance
10	40
10	70
10	82

5. Answers will vary. Students should note that a glide ratio is the ratio of height to (horizontal) distance. It tells you how far a glider can fly (in meters) if it is launched at a height of one meter.

Hints and Comments

Materials

centimeter rulers (one per student)

Overview

Students trace the flight path of a glider with a given steepness and determine how far the glider will fly if it is launched from a given height. They compare the performance of the glider with those of the gliders on page 33 of the Student Book. Students also explain what a glide ratio is.

Planning

Students may work on problem 4 individually. Discuss students' answers in class.

About the Mathematics

The term *glide ratio* is used in aviation as a measure for the performance of gliders. It is defined as the height-to-distance ratio.

Comments About the Solutions

4. a. When students trace the glider's path, make sure that they maintain the glider's steepness. Students can do this by aligning the notebook paper so that its edges are exactly lined up with the edges of the Student Book page, or so that its edges are parallel to the edges of the Student Book page. Students should draw the height and a line that represents the ground (and that intersects with the flight path). The height and the line that represents the ground should form a right angle.

5. Encourage students to write extensively about what they think a glide ratio is. Discuss students' answers. Be sure that all students understand the definition of glide ratio before they continue.

Notes

6 and 7 Students should draw pictures of these problems and make a ratio table.

6 Change glide ratios to decimals.

7 Note that distance is given, not height.

8 Students should use graph paper and draw these triangles to scale. Remind students to draw triangles large enough to get an accurate measurement of the angle. (On quarter-inch graph paper, a triangle with a ratio of 1:1 could be drawn as an 8:8.)

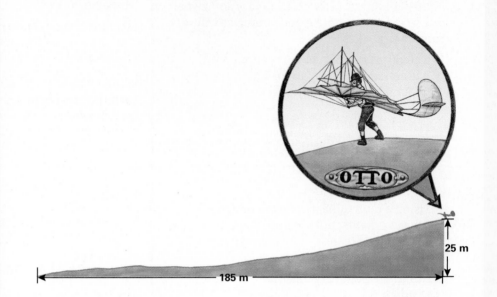

Otto Lilienthal made more than 2,000 flights with hang gliders at the end of the 19th century. Suppose that on one of his flights from the Rhinower Hills near Berlin, Germany, he started from a height of 25 m and covered 185 m of ground distance as shown here. On his next flight, suppose he redesigned his glider a little, started from a height of 20 m, and traveled a ground distance of 155 m.

6. What were the glide ratios of Otto's two gliders? Which glider could travel farther?

7. Suppose that a glider has a glide ratio of 1:8. It takes off from a cliff and covers 120 m of ground distance. How high is the cliff?

8. Make scale drawings to represent the following glide ratios.

   a. 1:1   **b.** 1:2   **c.** 1:4

   d. 1:10   **e.** 1:20

Assessment Pyramid

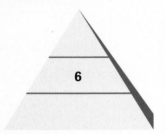

Make relative comparisons involving steepness problems and understand glide ratios.

Reaching All Learners

English Language Learners

Have students draw Lilienthal's flights and label the triangles.

Intervention

Ask, *What information is necessary to solve the Lilienthal problems? What information is unnecessary?*

Intervention

To practice, have students use 5 meters for the height and find the distance for Lilienthal's glider. Then they can use a height of 8 meters.

Solutions and Samples

6. 25:185 or 1:7.4 or about 1:7.

20:155 or 1:7.75 or about 1:8.

The second glider can travel farther because it has a slightly better glide ratio.

7. The cliff is 15 meters high. Students may use a ratio table:

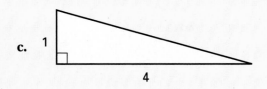

Height (in m)	1	10	5	15
Distance (in m)	8	80	40	120

+ column 2

8.

a.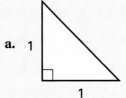

b.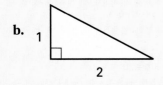

c.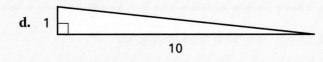

d.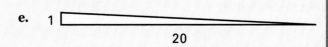

e. 1

20

Hints and Comments

Materials

centimeter rulers (one per student);
graph paper, optional (one sheet per student)

Overview

Students compare the performances of two gliders using glide ratios. They also make scale drawings showing the flight paths of gliders with given glide ratios.

Planning

Students may work on problems 6 and 7 in small groups. Students may do problem 8 individually. This problem can also be assigned as homework.

Comments About the Solutions

6. Students will need to simplify the ratios in order to compare the planes. Students may remember the process of simplifying ratios from the work they did in problem 4 on page 34 of the Student Book.

7. Students may use a ratio table to solve this problem.

8. This problem may be assigned as homework. You might want to have students use graph paper to make their scale drawings so they can align their right angles with the lines on the paper.

Did You Know?

Otto Lilienthal was an important aviation pioneer. Orville and Wilbur Wright, the brothers who built the first powered airplane that was capable of sustained flight, drew on the work of Otto Lilienthal. Before trying to build powered airplanes, the Wright brothers built three glider airplanes.

Notes

9 Discuss ways to express glide ratios. *Is it easier to compare fractions or decimals?*

Point out to students the similarities between the ladder and the glider situations.

9 Add another row to the chart labeled *h:d* (as a decimal).

10 Encourage students to solve this problem without using a calculator.

10 If students have difficulties, have them change all the ratios to decimals. Remind students that some of the ratios will not have a match.

In Section C when you studied ladders at different angles, you made a table similar to the one below, showing the angle between the ladder and the ground and the ratio of the height to the distance.

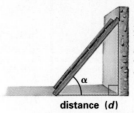

Ladder Steepness					
α	27°	30°	45°	60°	63°
h:d	0.5	0.6	1	1.7	2

You can organize your information about the steepness of the glide path of a hang glider with a similar table. The angle that the hang glider makes with the ground as it descends is called a **glide angle**.

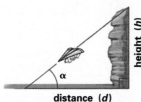

Glide Path Steepness					
Glide Angle α					
Glide Ratio h:d	1:1	1:2	1:4	1:10	1:20

9. Copy this table in your notebook. Fill in the missing glide angles by using the scale drawings you made for problem 8. Measure the angles using a compass card or protractor.

Glide ratios can also be expressed as fractions or decimals.

10. Which of the following glide ratios are equivalent?

   1:25 $\frac{4}{100}$ 1:20   3:75 $\frac{1}{20}$

   $\frac{1}{30}$ 2:40   0.04 $\frac{1}{25}$ 4:100

   0.05 $\frac{1}{4}$ 0.20   4:120 $\frac{2}{50}$

Assessment Pyramid

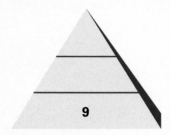

Measure angles.

Reaching All Learners

Vocabulary Building

Point out that equivalent means equal.

Accommodation

It may help students to have the ratios from problem 10 written on notecards to support the matching exercise.

Advanced Learner

Write ratios on cards. Each student receives a card and converts the ratio into a decimal. Students then order the cards from least to greatest, stacking the equivalent ratios.

Solutions and Samples

9.

Glide Path Steepness					
Glide Angle α	**45°**	**27°**	**14°**	**6°**	**3°**
Glide Ratio *h:d*	1:1	1:2	1:4	1:10	1:20

10. There are three different glide ratios with equivalent ratios: 1:25, 1:20 and 4:120. $\frac{1}{4}$ and 0.20 have no equivalents.

$1:25 = 3:75 = 4:100 = \frac{1}{25} = \frac{2}{50} = \frac{4}{100} = 0.04$.

$1:20 = 2:40 = \frac{1}{20} = 0.05$.

$4:120 = \frac{1}{30}$.

Hints and Comments

Materials

scientific calculators, optional (one per student or group of students)

Overview

Students make a table of the steepness of different flight paths using the information they gathered on page 35 of the Student Book. Also, they match equivalent glide ratios that are expressed as ratios, fractions, and decimals.

About the Mathematics

Students learned about equivalent ratios and fractions and about the relationships among ratios, fractions, and decimals in several MiC units in the Number strand. Make sure students are familiar with expressing ratios as fractions or percents.

Planning

Students may work on problems 9 and 10 in small groups. Have students compare their answers. You may want to discuss students' answers as a whole class.

Comments About the Solutions

9. For this problem, students will need the scale drawings they made for problem 8 on page 35 of the Student Book. If students' scale drawings are incorrect, their angle measures may also be inaccurate.

Extension

Glide ratios can also be expressed as percents. For example, $\frac{1}{5}$ and 0.20 are equivalent to 20%; 4:100, $\frac{1}{25}$, and 0.04 are equivalent to 4%; 1:30 is equivalent to $3\frac{1}{3}$%; and 1:20 is equivalent to 5%. You may want to have students express the ratios, fractions, and decimals given in problem 10 as percents.

Notes

11 Encourage students to solve this problem using the table from problem 9.

12 Remind students that the smaller the glide ratio, the safer the glider.

13 Read about tangent together. Ask students if they've ever seen the tan button on a calculator. Clarify problem 12 by having students complete the statement, "The greater the glide ratio, the (safer/more unsafe) the glider."

Suppose that it is safe to fly gliders that have a glide ratio smaller than 1:10.

11. What is the largest glide angle that is safe?

Suppose three gliders have the following glide ratios.

- Glider 1: 1:27
- Glider 2: 0.04
- Glider 3: $\frac{3}{78}$

12. Which glider is the safest? Explain.

From Glide Ratio to Tangent

The relationship between the glide ratio and the glide angle is very important in hang gliding, as well as in other applications, such as the placement of a ladder. For this reason, there are several ways to express this ratio and angle.

glide ratio = h:d

glide angle = α

The ratio h:d is also called the **tangent** of angle α, or $\tan \alpha = \frac{h}{d}$.

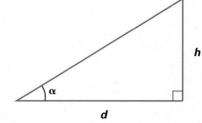

For a glide ratio of 1:1, the glide angle is 45°, so $\tan 45° = \frac{1}{1} = 1$.

Suppose that another one of Otto's hang gliders has a glide ratio of 1:7. This means that the tangent of the glide angle is 1 to 7 (or $\frac{1}{7}$).

13. Describe in your own words the relationship between the glide ratio, glide angle, and tangent.

Assessment Pyramid

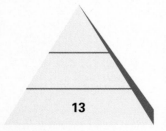

Understand the concept of glide ratio or tangent.

Reaching All Learners

Vocabulary Building

Tangent of alpha = height:distance.

Extension

Ask students, *How are the ladder problems and the glider problems similar?*

Intervention

For problem 11, check students' understanding of "a glide ratio smaller than 1:10." Ask students to give an example of a glide ratio smaller than 1:10. (For example, 1:100)

Ask students, *How would you compare the the glide angle for a glide ratio of 1:100 and the glide angle for a glide ratio of 1:10?*

Solutions and Samples

11. The largest glide angle that is safe is about 6°.

12. Glider 1 has the smallest glide angle, so it can travel farther than the other two gliders. The glider that can travel the farthest is also the safest.

In order to compare the gliders, students may write their glide ratios as decimals:

Glider 1   1:27 = 0.037

Glider 2   0.04

Glider 3 $\frac{3}{78}$ = 0.038

Or they may convert the decimal notations to glide ratios:

Glider 1   1:27

Glider 2   0.04 = 1:25

Glider 3 $\frac{3}{78}$ = 1:26

13. Descriptions will vary. Sample description:

The tangent is the same as the glide ratio; the ratio between the height a glider is launched from and the distance along the ground it flies. The glide angle is the angle between the flight path of a glider and the ground. The smaller the glide angle, the smaller the ratio between the height and the distance (or the glide ratio or tangent).

Hints and Comments

Materials

scientific calculators, optional (one per student or group of students)

Overview

Students compare the performances of gliders to determine which glider is the safest. Students also study a formal description of the concept of tangent. They are introduced to tangent notation.

About the Mathematics

At this point, what was known to students as "steepness" in the context of ladders or "glide ratio" in the context of gliders is formally named *tangent*. The tangent is the ratio of vertical height to horizontal distance in any context that can be represented with a right triangle.

Planning

Problems 11 and 12 may be done in small groups. Discuss students' answers in class. You may want to read and discuss the bottom half of this page together with students. Encourage students to ask questions and discuss anything that may be unclear to them. Students will use formal tangent notation throughout the rest of this section.

Comments About the Solutions

11. Any angle smaller than six degrees is safe, since it means that the glider will travel a long distance. A glider flying at a very steep angle is more likely to crash.

12. Students should realize that they will have to convert all the glide ratios to decimals or ratios in order to compare them.

Notes

Suppose that a glider follows the flight path shown here.

From this information, you know that the glide ratio of a 35° angle is 0.7 (or 7:10). You can write this information in the following way.

$\tan 35° = \frac{7}{10} = 0.7$

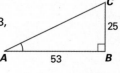

Here is a different glider situation.

You know the tangent of angle A is 25:53, or 0.47.

You can write this information in the following way.

$\tan A = \frac{25}{53} = 0.47$

14 The tangent of an angle describes the height-to-distance ratio and can be expressed as a fraction, decimal, or ratio. Remind students that tangent is always height over distance.

14. Complete the statements below for each of the following right triangles.

a. tan _?°_ = _?_   **b.** tan _?°_ = _?_

c. tan _?°_ = _?_   **d.** tan _?°_ = _?_

Reaching All Learners

Intervention

Relate these problems to the distance the hang gliders traveled and the distance the ladder was from the wall.

Reflection

Ask, *How does the angle size affect the ratio (tangent)?*

Solutions and Samples

14. a. tan 27° = 1:2, or 0.5

    b. tan 45° = 1:1, or 1

    c. tan 63° = 2:1, or 2

    d. tan 72° = 3:1, or 3

Hints and Comments

Overview

Students study formal tangent notation. Then they find the tangents of angles in four right triangles.

Planning

Students should read the text at the top of the page carefully. Students may work on problem 14 individually. Discuss students' answers in class.

Comments About the Solutions

14. This problem is meant for students to become familiar with and practice formal tangent notation. They do not have to calculate or measure. They may refer to the example at the top of the page to see how statements like these are written. Note: The measurements shown in the Solutions column are approximations. For example, tan 63° is closer to 1.9626 than to 2.

Notes

16 Review how to name sides of a triangle. Students should use graph paper to easily make scale drawings.

17 Draw these triangles reasonably. It's not necessary to draw them exactly to scale.

Students should add the dimensions for height and distance to their drawings.

19 Rephrase this problem to: "How far is the ladder from the wall, and what is the height of the ladder up the wall?" Draw this triangle.

Peter wants to buy a balsa wood model glider for his nephew, but he is not sure which one to buy. The salesperson at the hobby store claims, "The smaller the tangent of the glide angle, the better the glider."

15. Is the salesperson correct? Explain.

16. Suppose for triangle *ABC*, the measure of angle *B* is 90° and $\tan A = \frac{3}{5}$.

   a. Make a scale drawing of triangle *ABC*.

   b. Suppose you drew triangle *ABC* so that side *AB* measures 10 cm. What is the length of side *BC*?

   c. What is the measure of angle *A* in triangle *ABC*? Is it the same size in both of the triangles drawn?

The following table lists some angles and the approximate measurements of their tangents.

Angle (in degrees)	0°	1°	2°	3°	4°	5°	31°	32°	33°	34°	35°
Tangent of Angle (as a decimal)	0	0.02	0.04	0.05	0.07	0.09	0.60	0.63	0.65	0.68	0.70

Use the table to answer the following problems.

17. a. Draw a side view of the flight path for a glider whose glide angle is 5°.

   b. What is the glide ratio for this glider?

18. If the glide angle is 35°, how much ground distance does a glider cover from a height of 100 m?

19. If a ladder makes an 80° angle with the ground, what can you determine about the position of the ladder if you know tan 80° = 5.7?

Assessment Pyramid

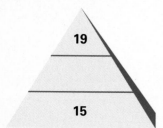

19

15

Solve problems involving right triangle trigonometry ratios.
Understand the concept of glide ratio, or tangent.

Reaching All Learners

Extension

You might ask students to comment on the following statement: "The smaller the glide angle, the better the glider." Have students compare this statement to the one made by the salesperson on page 39 of the Student Book.

Solutions and Samples

15. Yes, the salesperson is correct. Explanations will vary. Sample explanation:

The smaller the tangent of the glide angle, the better the glide ratio. For instance, a glide ratio of 1:20 means that for every meter of launching height, the glider will cover 20 meters on the ground. A smaller glide ratio such as 1:200 means that the glider covers 200 meters on the ground if it is launched from a height of 1 meter. This would be a spectacular distance to travel with such a take-off height, obviously a better glider!

16. a.

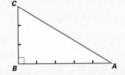

b. Side *BC* would measure 6 centimeters.

Many students will know the distance is doubled and will not need to use a ratio table here.

c. Angle *A* measures about 31°. Yes, angle *A* is the same size in both triangles.

17. a. Sample explanation:

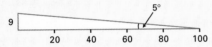

b. 9:100. The table shows that for an angle of 5°, the tangent is 0.09, which is 9 hundredths. This is written as 9:100. Therefore, when the glider is launched from a height of 9 meters, it covers a ground distance of 100 meters.

18. 143 meters.

If the glide angle is 35°, the table shows the tangent is 0.70 or 7:10; when the glider takes off from a height of 7 meters, it covers 10 meters of ground distance.

Here is a ratio table solution:

	× 100		÷ 7
Height (in m)	7	700	100
Distance (in m)	10	1,000	≈ 143

19. Answers will vary. Sample response:

The ladder reaches 5.7 meters up the wall if the bottom of the ladder is 1 meter away from the wall, as shown here.

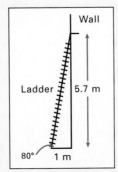

Hints and Comments

Materials

centimeter rulers (one per student);
protractors or compass cards (one per student);
scientific calculators, optional (one per student)

Overview

Students investigate how the tangent of the glide angle affects the performance of a glider. They also make scale drawings of right triangles. When the glide angle is given, students find the tangent, and vice versa. They use a table of angles and their corresponding tangents to solve problems.

Planning

Students may work on problem 15 individually. Discuss students' answers in class. Then students can continue working on problems 16–19 in small groups or individually. Discuss their answers in class.

Comments About the Solutions

15. Students must realize that a glider with a small glide ratio or tangent will fly relatively far (considering the height).

16. a. There are several possibilities for making a scale drawing of the triangle. Any scale drawing is acceptable as long as the ratio between height and distance is 3:5. Make sure students label vertices *A*, *B*, and *C* correctly.

b. If the distance is multiplied by two, the height must also be multiplied by two to maintain the same height-to-distance ratio.

c. No matter what size students' drawings are, they should find that the angle measures about 31°.

17. a. Students may first draw the 5° angle and then complete the triangle. The length of the distance they choose is not important, but it will be easier to find the height-to-distance ratio if students choose a convenient length.

b. Students can find the glide ratio by measuring the height and distance of the triangle they drew. But it is easier to use the table on page 39 of the Student Book.

19. This problem assesses students' ability to understand the contexts involving steepness that may be represented with a right triangle. Be sure students understand that the tangent ratio relates to triangles formed in many contexts, such as gliding, ladders leaning against walls, vision lines on boats, and so on.

D Glide Angles

Notes

For many students, a scientific calculator is a mysterious "black box." In the beginning, students will benefit from using the table in the Appendix, which will help them make sense of the relationship between the angle and tangent ratios.

20 Students should be able to give the height and distance of triangles with the given glide angles.

21 This is an important tangent value to remember; you might call it a benchmark tangent value. You may ask students what they know about the tangent values for angles smaller than 45° and larger than 45°.

The table in Appendix A shows the relationship between the size of an angle and its tangent value. You can also use a scientific calculator to find the tangent of an angle. Since calculators differ, you may want to investigate how to use the tangent key on your calculator. You can use the table in the appendix to verify your work.

You can also use a scientific calculator to find angle measurements if you know the tangent ratio.

Use either the table or the tangent key on your scientific calculator to answer the following problems.

20. What do you know about a glider with a glide angle of 4°? A glide angle of 35°?

21. Explain why tan 45° = 1.

22. Which angle has a tangent value of 2? Of 3? Of 4?

23. How much does the measurement of the angle change when the tangent value changes in these ways?

    a. From 0 to 1

    b. From 1 to 2

    c. From 2 to 3

    d. From 3 to 4

    e. From 4 to 5

Assessment Pyramid

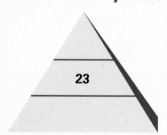

23

Understand the relationship among steepness, angle, and height-to-distance ratio.

Reaching All Learners

Intervention

Give students various sizes of squares and have them cut them apart across the diagonal. Students should see that the triangles are congruent. Have them measure the three angles. Students should discover the two 45° angles have equal opposite sides. Because of that property of triangles, the tangent of 45° is always 1.

Solutions and Samples

20. Answers will vary. Sample responses:

   A glider with a glide angle of 4° has a tangent of 0.070, or a glide ratio of 7:100. This glider can travel 100 meters when it is launched from a height of 7 meters.

   A glider with a glide angle of 35° has a tangent of 0.700, or a glide ratio of 7:10. This glider is dangerous. If it is launched from a height of 7 meters, it will fly only 10 meters.

21. The tangent of 45° is equal to 1 because the height and distance in a right triangle with two 45° angles are equal. The ratio is 1:1, so the tangent is $\frac{1}{1}$ or 1.

22. An angle of about 63° or 64° has a tangent of 2.

   An angle of about 71° or 72° has a tangent of 3.

   An angle of about 76° has a tangent of 4.

23. **a.** The measure of the angle changes by 45°. When the tangent value is 0, the angle measures 0°; when the tangent value is 1, the angle measures 45°. The difference is 45°.

   b. The measure of the angle changes by 18°. When the tangent value is 1, the angle measures 45°; when the tangent value is 2, the angle measures about 63°. The difference is 18°.

   c. The measure of the angle changes by 8°. When the tangent value is 2, the angle measures about 63°; when the tangent value is 3, the angle measures about 71°. The difference is 8°.

   d. The measure of the angle changes by 5°. When the tangent value is 3, the angle measures about 71°; when the tangent value is 4, the angle measures 76°. The difference is 5°.

   e. The measure of the angle changes by 3°. When the tangent value is 4, the angle measures 76°; when the tangent value is 5, the angle measures about 79°. The difference is 3°.

Hints and Comments

Materials

Appendix A on Teacher's Guide pages 61A–62 (Student Book pages 68–70); scientific calculators, optional (one per student)

Overview

Students find angle measures for tangent values and vice versa, using a scientific calculator or a tangent table.

Planning

Introduce the tangent table from Appendix A or the tangent key on a scientific calculator in class. Make sure all students understand how to use one or both. Students will need to use the tangent table or a scientific calculator to solve the remaining problems in this section. Students may work on problems 20–23 in small groups. Discuss their answers in class.

Comments About the Solutions

20. Students may find the corresponding glide ratios in the tangent table (or by using a calculator) and reason from there.

22. and 23.
   The purpose of these problems is to familiarize students with the use of the tangent table or the tangent key on a scientific calculator.

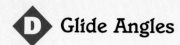
Math History

Shadows and Gliders

Shadow reckoning was an early device for finding heights. If you see the sun's rays under an angle of 45°, you can measure the shadow of a tower to know its height.

Around 400 B.C., the Hindus understood the use of shadows to measure heights. Albategnius made the first *tables of shadows* around 920 A.D.

Around 860, the first table of *tangents* was constructed by the Arabs (Habash-al-Hasib). Arab writers described the straight shadow *umbra recta* (horizontal distance) and the turned shadow or *umbra versa* (vertical distance).

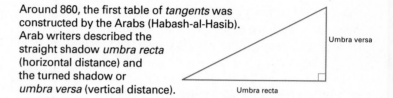

As soon as the first glider planes were invented, their performances were compared by using glide ratios. The German aviator Otto Lilienthal (around 1890) made a kind of hang glider with glide ratios of around 1 to 9, which is also the glide ratio of NASA's space shuttle.

There is always confusion about glide ratios: In Europe, people identify 1:40 as the glide ratio of a good contemporary sailplane (sometimes even 1:60!), but in the United States you can often see 42:1 or even just 42.

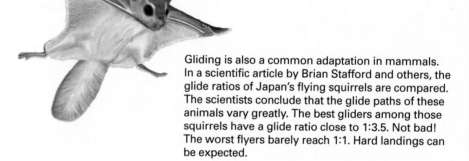

Gliding is also a common adaptation in mammals. In a scientific article by Brian Stafford and others, the glide ratios of Japan's flying squirrels are compared. The scientists conclude that the glide paths of these animals vary greatly. The best gliders among those squirrels have a glide ratio close to 1:3.5. Not bad! The worst flyers barely reach 1:1. Hard landings can be expected.

Reaching All Learners

Advanced Learners

Encourage students to search the Internet to find descriptions of the various applications of glide ratio. Have them report their findings to the rest of the class.

Hints and Comments

Overview

You may want to have students read this page and discuss it in class. It is optional.

Glide Angles

Notes

1 Students should show equivalent ratios for this problem.

D Glide Angles

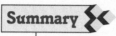

Summary

The steepness of a ladder, the angle of the sun's rays, and the flight path of a hang glider can all be modeled by a right triangle such as the one here.

Steepness can be measured as the angle α or as the ratio $h{:}d$.

The ratio $h{:}d$ is also called the tangent of angle α, or $\tan \alpha = \frac{h}{d}$.

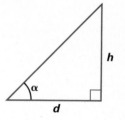

Check Your Work

On a calm day, a glider pilot wants to make a flight that covers 120 km. The glider has a glide ratio of 1:40.

1. From what height does the glider have to be launched?

Assessment Pyramid

Assesses Section D Goals

Reaching All Learners

Intervention

For more practice, use an example of two glide ratios such as 7:10 and 2:5. What are the alpha angles?

Solutions and Samples

Answers to Check Your Work

1. The glider must be launched from a height of 3 km.

   Since the glide ratio is 1:40, and 120 is three times 40 km, you only need to triple the height.

Hints and Comments

Overview

Students read the Summary, which reviews the main concepts covered in this section. Students use the Check Your Work problems as self-assessment. The answers to these problems are also provided on pages 65 and 66 of the Student Book. After students complete Section D, you may assign as homework appropriate activities from the Additional Practice section, located on pages 58 and 59 of the Student Book. After students have completed Sections C and D, you may use Quiz 2 as a mid-unit assessment.

About the Mathematics

The Summary of this section outlines the main mathematical concepts of Sections A–D. Each context that was featured in these sections may be represented with a right triangle: steepness of the vision line, steepness of the sun's rays, steepness of the ladder, and steepness of the glide path. Each serves to establish understanding of the tangent concept. Students may always remember the tangent as the "glide ratio" of a glider.

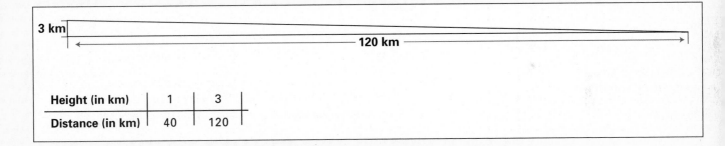

Height (in km)	1	3
Distance (in km)	40	120

Notes

2 Students may need to lbe reminded that there are 1,000 meters in a kilometer.

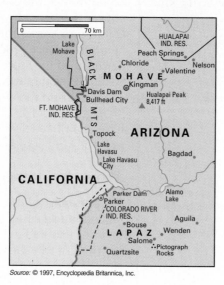

Source: © 1997, Encyclopædia Britannica, Inc.

A glider with a glide ratio of 1:28 is launched after being pulled by an airplane to 1,200 m above Lake Havasu City in Arizona.

2. Indicate on the map on **Student Activity Sheet 11** how far the glider can fly if there is no wind.

Here are some of the right triangles you worked with in problem 14.

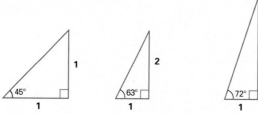

You used tangent notation to describe each situation:

a. tan 45° = 1   **b.** tan 63° = 2   **c.** tan 72° = 3

3. **a.** Suppose these right triangles were ladder situations. What conclusions can you make about these ladders?

   b. What can you conclude about the length of a ladder described by tan 86° = 14?

3a Students should explain whether the ladders would be safe or unsafe.

3b Students should draw this triangle or reason.

Assessment Pyramid

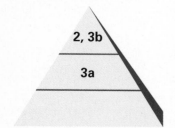

Assesses Section D Goals

Reaching All Learners

Intervention

For problem 2, if students draw only one location for the glider to land, ask them whether there is another possible landing location, and repeat this question until they realize that they can indicate all possible landing locations by drawing a circle.

Solutions and Samples

2. The distance the glider can go is 33,600 m or 33.6 km.

Here is a ratio table with the 1:28 glide ratio, building up to 1,200 m height.

Height (in km)	1	10	1,000	20	200	1,200
Distance (in km)	28	280	28,000	560	5,600	33,600

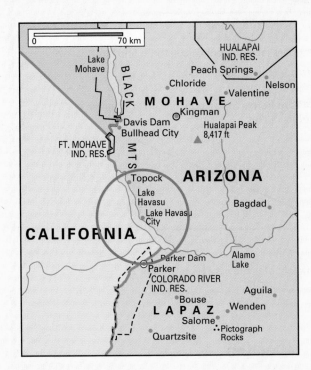

Using the map scale line, you should draw a circle around Lake Havasu City.

3. a. Some students will focus on the ladder position on the wall; others might focus on the relative lengths of the ladders. As the ladder was moved higher up the wall, the angle at the base increased. If you want to keep the ladder 1 m from the wall, then you need to get taller and taller ladders to make the specified angle.

b. The length of the ladder is probably greater than 14 m. If the height is 14 m when the ladder is 1 meter from the wall. The ladder should always be greater than the height along the wall.

Hints and Comments

Materials
Student Activity Sheet 11

Overview
Students use the Check Your Work problems as self-assessment.

◆ **D** Glide Angles

A road has been constructed with a fairly large angle between the road and the horizontal plane.

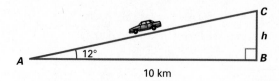

4. a. Use the tangent table or your calculator to find tan 12°.

   b. Use this to compute height *h*.

At a distance of 160 m from a tower, you look up at an angle of 23° and see the top of the tower.

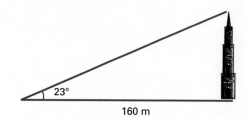

5. What is the height of the tower? Hint: Use tan 23°.

◆ **For Further Reflection**

For Further Reflection

This type of reflective question supports student summarization of important concepts from this section.

Write a short paragraph about the similarities you see between the situations involving ladders and hang gliders. In your description, use the terms *steepness, height-to-distance ratio*, and *angle*.

Assessment Pyramid

Assesses Section D Goals

Reaching All Learners

Intervention

Students may need help getting problem 4 set up: tan 12° = height/10 km.

Solutions and Samples

4. a. tan 12° = 0.21.

   b. 2.1 km.

   Strategies may vary. Sample strategy:

   tan 12° = 0.21, which means that you need a height of 21 km to travel 100 km. The car needs to descend a ground distance of 10 km, so I only need to divide 21 by 10 to get an answer of 2.1 km. This keeps the same glide ratio and angle of 12°.

5. 67.2 m.

   Sample strategy:

   tan 23° = 0.42, which means that you need a height of 42 m to travel 100 m along the ground. Then I used a ratio table and placed the glide ratio in the first column. My goal was to build up to a distance of 160 m.

Height (in m)	42	21	4.2	67.2		
Distance (in m)	100	50	10	160		

For Further Reflection

Answers will vary. Sample response:

Situations involving ladders and hang gliders can be represented with a right triangle:

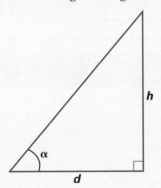

h stands for the height reached by the ladder or the height a glider is launched from; *d* stands for the distance between the ladder and the wall or the distance a glider flies.

If you want to indicate the steepness of the ladder or the flight path of the glider, you can use the height-to-distance ratio: the bigger the ratio, the steeper the ladder or the flight path of the glider. You can also look at the angle **α**: The larger the angle, the steeper the ladder or the flight path of the glider.

Hints and Comments

Overview

Students use the Check Your Work problems as self-assessment. They may reflect on Sections C and D by answering the For Further Reflection problem.

Comments About the Solutions

For Further Reflection

You may want to encourage students to include drawings in their writing. Make sure that they add labels to their drawings showing what is represented.

Section Focus

The instructional focus of Section E is to:

• reflect on the different contexts in this unit and find commonalities;

• review the concept of tangent and relate the concept of slope to tangent;

• review the Pythagorean theorem;

• learn about the sine and cosine and use formal notation for tangent, sine, and cosine;

• use a sine and cosine table or the sine and cosine keys on a scientific calculator; and

• use tangent, sine, cosine and the Pythagorean theorem to solve problems.

Pacing and Planning

Day 17: Tangent Ratio		Student pages 45–50
INTRODUCTION	Problems 1 and 2	Read about the flying method used by vultures and compare the glide ratio of a vulture to that of a glider.
CLASSWORK	Problems 3–6c	Use the Pythagorean theorem to find missing side lengths of right triangles and to calculate the length of a vulture's flight path.
HOMEWORK	Problems 6d–7	Solve problems using the tangent ratio and the Pythagorean theorem.

Day 18: The Ratios: Tangent, Sine, and Cosine		Student pages 50–55
INTRODUCTION	Review homework.	Review homework from Day 17.
CLASSWORK	Problems 8–14	Investigate and apply sine, cosine, and tangent.
HOMEWORK	Check Your Work For Further Reflection	Student self-assessment: Solve problems using sine, cosine, and tangent.

Additional Resources: Additional Practice, Section E, Student Book page 60

Materials

Student Resources

Quantities listed are per student.

- Appendix A on Teacher's Guide pages 61A–62 (Student Book pages 68–70)

Teachers Resources

No resources required

Student Materials

Quantities listed are per student.

- Calculators

- Protractors or compass cards

* See Hints and Comments for optional materials.

Learning Lines

Pythagorean Theorem

In the unit *Triangles and Beyond*, the Pythagorean theorem was introduced. It is briefly reviewed in this section, where students learn that it can be written as an equation, $a^2 + b^2 = c^2$, where a and b represent the two smallest sides of a right triangle, and c represents the longest side. The term *hypotenuse* is used for the first time in this unit, but the concept is not new since students are familiarized with it as being the flight path or the ladder. The Pythagorean theorem can be used to find the length of any one side of a right triangle if the lengths of the other two sides are known. This becomes quite useful for solving problems involving ratios between the sides of right triangles (i.e., tangent, sine, cosine).

Slope

In the unit *Graphing Equations*, slope was introduced as the ratio of the vertical component to the horizontal component. The slope of a line gives the direction of a line, which is a measure of how steep it is. In the unit *Graphing Equations*, students also investigated if the tangent of the angle that a line makes with the positive (or right) side of the *x*-axis is equal to the slope. This is only the case if both the horizontal and the vertical axis are scaled in the same way. The tangent of an angle is similarly defined as the vertical distance divided by the horizontal distance. Students also discovered that the slope is not proportional to the angle.

In Section E of this unit, the concept of slope is revised as a measure for the steepness of a glider's flight path. It is the same as the glide ratio. In summary:

- α = glide angle
- $\tan \alpha = \frac{h}{d}$
- glide ratio = $h{:}d$ or $\frac{h}{d}$
- slope = $h{:}d$ or $\frac{h}{d}$

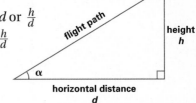

Tangent, Sine, Cosine

The concept of tangent was carefully developed in this unit, using several contexts that serve as a model. When students need to know what tangent is, they only need to remind themselves that it is the same as the glide ratio: the ratio of the height the glider is launched from to the horizontal distance it covers. After the formalization process of the concept of tangent is completed, sine and cosine are introduced at a formal level, as being two other ratios, which describe a relationship between two sides of a right triangle. In summary:

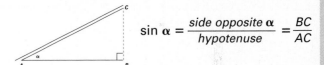

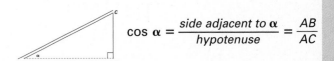

At the End of this Section: Learning Outcomes

Students understand the concept of tangent and slope at a formal level. Students know what the sine and cosine ratios mean, they can use formal sine and cosine notation, and they can find sine and cosine values when solving problems. Students also know how to use the Pythagorean theorem to solve problems involving the lengths of the sides of a right triangle.

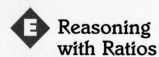
Notes

Use this page to review the
content of the unit so far
with your students.

Reasoning with Ratios

Tangent Ratio

So far, you have worked with situations like these.

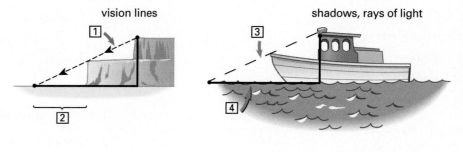

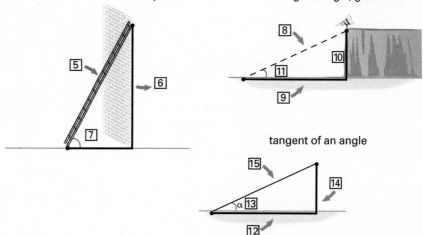

1. The elements of these situations are labeled with numbers from
   1 to 15. Name each element. For example, a line labeled with a
   number might be a ray of light or a flight path.

Reaching All Learners

Extension

Some students may need a word bank from the solution for problem 1.

Word bank: height, distance, height of cliff, height up wall, distance from
wall, ground distance, hypotenuse, ladder, glider path, glide angle, blind
area, blind spot, vision line, ladder angle.

Solutions and Samples

1.
   1 vision line
   2 blind spot
   3 light ray
   4 shadow (or blind spot)
   5 ladder
   6 height reached by the ladder on the wall
   7 angle indicating steepness of ladder
   8 flight path
   9 ground distance flown
   10 height the glider is launched from
   11 glide angle
   12 distance
   13 angle
   14 height
   15 hypotenuse

Hints and Comments

Overview

Students review the mathematical content of the previous sections.

About the Mathematics

On this page, the different contexts students have seen in the unit are summarized. Notice that each of these contexts can be represented with a right triangle. Also, in each context the concept of steepness is important.

Planning

Have students work on problem 1 individually and discuss the results in class.

Reasoning with Ratios

Notes

All the situations on the previous page have a right triangle in common. In many situations, the ratio of the height to distance plays an important role, $\tan \alpha = \frac{h}{d}$.

This ratio is a measurement for *steepness*, as is the angle. A small angle corresponds to low steepness.

Vultures Versus Gliders

2a Encourage students to sketch right triangles for the vulture's glide path and the glider's path.

Refer to page 39 for a definition of a better glider. The smaller the tangent of the glide angle, the better the glide.

Note: The Vultures vs. Gliders paragraph contains additional unnecessary information.

While searching for food, vultures use updraft hot air currents, or thermals, to gain altitude. They rise up circling and after reaching a certain altitude, glide down to catch a new thermal column. Vultures look for thermals so that they can gain altitude without expending energy. Like vultures, gliders also rely on thermals.

Vultures and gliders can be compared in terms of their glide ratios.

For the vulture, the glide ratio is 1:10, or $\tan \alpha = 0.1$.

For the glider, $\tan \alpha = 0.03$.

2. **a.** Who is the better "glider?"

   b. What distance can each fly, starting from a vertical height of 1 km?

   c. What is the size of the two glide angles?

   d. Which flight path is steeper?

2c Students can use Appendix A on Student Book pages 68–70 or scientific calculators to determine the glide angles using the glide ratios.

Assessment Pyramid

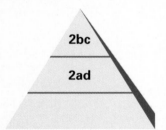

2bc

2ad

Understand when contexts can be represented by a right triangle.
Make relative comparisons involving steepness.

Reaching All Learners

Intervention

Review method of converting between decimals and fractions and how to compare the glide ratios as fractions.

Solutions and Samples

2. a. The glider is better because it doesn't have to be up as high as the vulture to cover the same distance along the ground.

vulture: 1:10

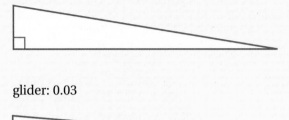

glider: 0.03

b. vulture: 10 km (glide ratio is 1:10)

glider: 33 km (glide ratio is 3:100, which is about 1:33)

c. vulture: about 6°

tan α = 0.1 then $\alpha \approx 5.7°$ or 6°

glider: about 2°

tan α = 0.03 then $\alpha \approx 1.7°$ or 2°

d. The vulture has a steeper flight path.

Hints and Comments

Materials

Appendix A on Teacher's Guide pages 61A–62 (Student Book pages 68–70); scientific calculator (one per student);

Overview

Students may read the conclusions to be drawn from the previous page. Students read about the flying method used by vultures and compare the glide ratio of a vulture to that of a glider. Students will again encounter vultures in problem 5 of this section.

Planning

You may have students read the text at the top of the page and the text about vultures and gliders before they start working on problem 2. This problem may be done in small groups. Use this problem to assess if students understand the concepts of glide ratio, glide angle and steepness.

Did You Know?

Vultures use various methods of flight. They can beat or flap their wings, or they can hover and remain suspended in the air. Vultures are large birds, so they generally flap their wings only to begin flight or to move from perch to perch. Once airborne, they need large thermals to support their weight. The Old World black vulture is one of the biggest and heaviest birds of flight. It weighs about 12.5 kilograms (27.5 pounds), is about 100 centimeters (39 inches) long and has a wingspan of about 2.7 meters (9 feet).

Reasoning with Ratios

Notes

The Pythagorean theorem was introduced in the unit *Triangles and Beyond*.

Pythagoras

You may remember a theorem that is closely connected to right triangles. It is called the **Pythagorean theorem**. Pythagoras was born in Samos, Ionia, in the sixth century B.C. The Pythagorean theorem is used to calculate the length of any one side of a right triangle if the lengths of the other two sides are known.

If a triangle has a right angle, then the square on the longest side has the same area as the other two combined.

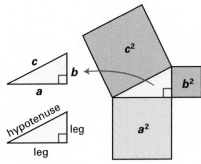

You can write the Pythagorean theorem as an equation, $a^2 + b^2 = c^2$, where a and b represent the two short sides, called **legs**, of a right triangle, and c represents the longest side, called the **hypotenuse**. The hypotenuse is always the side opposite the right angle.

Reaching All Learners

Vocabulary

Hypotenuse: the side opposite the right angle of a right triangle (also the longest side). In the context we have used so far, it is the vision line, the light ray, the ladder, and the flight path.

Pythagorean theorem: $a^2 + b^2 = c^2$. This only applies to right triangles!

Hands-On Learning

Have students take graph paper and cut out squares of 3×3, 4×4, and 5×5. Discuss the relationship between the area of a square and squaring. Show that the area of the two smaller squares will fit into the larger square. This will help students recall "squaring" and how the Pythagorean theorem works.

Hints and Comments

Overview

Students read about the Pythagorean theorem.

About the Mathematics

The Pythagorean theorem is used to find to find a missing side of a right triangle given the lengths of the other two sides. Make sure students understand that the theorem applies only to right triangles. The term hypotenuse is used for the first time in the unit. Make sure students understand what it means. You may refer to contexts they have seen before in which the hypotenuse could be the vision line, the light ray, the ladder or the flight path.

Planning

You may read the text on this page and discuss it in class. Make sure students understand the drawing at the bottom of the page and explain what the equation shows.

With this picture story you may need to point out to students that they should follow the arrows from one picture to the next.

If you know the measurements of all three sides of a triangle, you can use the Pythagorean theorem to find out whether the triangle is a right triangle. If $a^2 + b^2 \neq c^2$, then the triangle is not a right triangle.

The Pythagorean theorem is used to find distances. Look carefully at the following picture story.

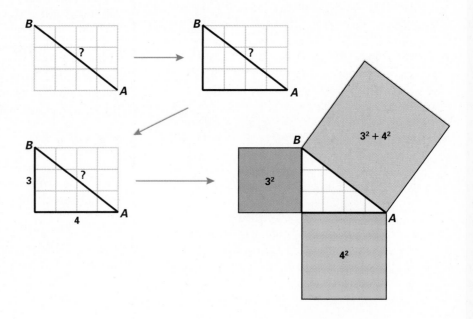

3a Encourage students to explain the story orally before they begin writing. Make sure students read through the picture story, like a comic.

3b Remind students to find the square root of 25.

3. **a.** Explain the picture story.

 b. What is the length of segment *AB*?

Reaching All Learners

Accommodation

Give students graph paper and have them prove the picture story by reallotting the two smaller squares to make the larger one.

Intervention

If students are having trouble getting started on problem 3a, have them go back to page 45 which shows all the situations we have talked about, and choose one of those to use for the story.

Solutions and Samples

3. a. Explanations will vary. Sample explanation:

The first picture shows a rectangular part of a grid, for which *AB* is a diagonal. The second picture shows how a right triangle can be made, with *AB* as its longest side. The third picture labels the lengths of the two shorter sides: 3 units and 4 units. The last picture shows squares drawn from each of the three sides of the right triangle. The areas of the two smaller squares were found by squaring the sides. Since the area of the largest square of a right triangle is the same as the sum of the areas of the two smaller squares, we now know the area of the largest square. By taking the square root of this area, we can find the length of longest side of the triangle, the length of line segment *AB*.

b. Segment *AB* is 5 units long, since $3^2 + 4^2 = 9 + 16 = 25$, and $\sqrt{25} = 5$.

Hints and Comments

Overview

Students read how they can find out whether a triangle is a right triangle. They also learn how the Pythagorean theorem can be used to find distances and use this knowledge to find missing side lengths of right triangles.

About the Mathematics

Students should be able to explain why the formula $a^2 + b^2 = c^2$ works so that they can use it to solve problems.

Planning

Students may read the text and work on problem 3 in small groups. Discuss the results in class.

Comments About the Solutions

3. a. Use this problem to assess if students understand the Pythagorean theorem. They will need it to solve problems throughout the remainder of this section.

Reasoning with Ratios

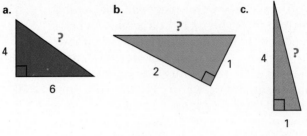

Notes

4 Before using a calculator, encourage students to estimate the size of a square root, such as $\sqrt{52}$, by locating the two perfect squares the square falls between (49 and 64). In this way, students will see that a side length of $\sqrt{52}$ is shorter than 8, but longer than 7. Since $49 < 52 < 64$, this can be written as $7 < \sqrt{52} < 8$.

4d and 4f Some students may find these problems more challenging since the length of leg is missing, rather than the length of the hypotenuse.

5a Some students may want to use a ratio table.

5b Students may use Appendix A on Student Book pages 68–70 instead of a calculator.

5c Students should estimate the square root, but will then need a calculator to find a more precise estimate of the square root.

4. Find the missing distances in the triangles below. Show your work.

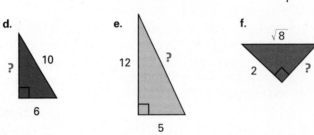

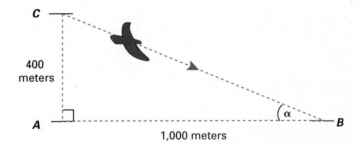

The vulture does not have to fly at a glide ratio of 1:10. It can glide at much steeper angles, especially when diving for food.

5. a. What is the vulture's glide ratio in the picture above?

b. Use your calculator to find the size of the glide angle.

c. Use the Pythagorean theorem to calculate the length of the vulture's flight path (*BC*).

Assessment Pyramid

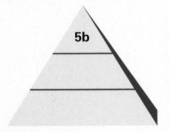

5b

Solve problems with right triangle trigonometry ratios.

Reaching All Learners

Intervention

Some students may find it difficult to solve these problems using equations. It may be helpful to explain the following strategy instead:

Side Length	Area
4	16
6	32
$\sqrt{52}$	52

Solutions and Samples

4. a. The missing distance is about 7.2.

$$a^2 + b^2 = c^2$$
$$4^2 + 6^2 = c^2$$
$$16 + 36 = c^2$$
$$52 = c^2$$
$$\sqrt{52} = c$$
$$c \approx 7.2$$

b. The missing distance is about 2.2.

$$a^2 + b^2 = c^2$$
$$1^2 + 2^2 = c^2$$
$$5 = c^2$$
$$\sqrt{5} = c$$
$$c \approx 2.2$$

c. The missing distance is about 4.1.

$$a^2 + b^2 = c^2$$
$$1^2 + 4^2 = c^2$$
$$17 = c^2$$
$$\sqrt{17} = c$$
$$c \approx 4.1$$

d. The missing distance is 8.

$$a^2 + b^2 = c^2$$
$$6^2 + b^2 = 100$$
$$36 + b^2 = 100$$
$$b^2 = 100 - 36$$
$$b^2 = 64$$
$$b = \sqrt{64} = 8$$

e. The missing distance is 13.

$$a^2 + b^2 = c^2$$
$$5^2 + 12^2 = c^2$$
$$25 + 144 = c^2$$
$$169 = c^2$$
$$\sqrt{169} = c$$
$$c = 13$$

f. The missing distance is 2.

$$a^2 + b^2 = c^2$$
$$2^2 + b^2 = (\sqrt{8})^2$$
$$4 + b^2 = 8$$
$$b^2 = 8 - 4$$
$$b^2 = 4$$
$$b = \sqrt{4} = 2$$

Hints and Comments

Materials

Appendix A on Teacher's Guide pages 61A–62 (Student Book pages 68–70); scientific calculator (one per student)

Overview

Students use the Pythagorean theorem to find missing side lengths of right triangles. They also use this theorem to calculate the length of a vulture's flight path.

Planning

You may have students work on problem 4 individually and use it for informal assessment. Problem 5 can be completed in small groups.

Comments About the Solutions

4. You may use this problem to assess students' ability to use the Pythagorean theorem.

5. a. The glide ratio is 1:2.5. In a ratio table:

height (in m)	400	4	2	1
distance (in m)	1,000	10	5	2.5

b. The glide angle is about 22°.

Sample calculation:

$\tan \alpha = 0.4$ so α is about 22°.

c. The vulture's flight path is about 1,077 m.

Using the Pythagorean theorem:

$$400^2 + 1,000^2 = \text{Path}^2$$
$$160,000 + 1,000,000 = \text{Path}^2$$
$$1,160,000 = \text{Path}^2$$

The path is $\sqrt{1,160,000} \approx 1,077$ m.

E Reasoning with Ratios

Notes

6c Remind students to apply the Pythagorean theorem.

6d This problem states that the triangles should be similar. You may wish to have students try to make this triangle to prove why it won't work.

You may want to encourage students to try and draw this right triangle to get them started. You may need to point out that in the drawing $AB = 5$ cm, representing a length of 1,000 m in reality. To find the length of AC, students will need the tangent table; to find the length of BC, they need to apply the Pythagorean theorem.

7a Make sure students note the scale they used for their drawing. (1 cm represents 1 m is an appropriate scale.)

7b This problem introduces cosine, but students use a scale drawing to measure the distance from the wall.

If the glide angle is very small, lengths AB and BC will be like they are in problem 5. What happens if the glide angle is greater?

Consider a right triangle with an angle of 40°.

6. **a.** Use a ruler and a protractor to draw a right triangle ABC. Angle A is the right angle, angle $B = 40°$, and the length of $AB = 5$ cm. AB represents a length of 1,000 m in reality.

   b. Use your calculator or the appendix to find tan 40° and calculate the length of AC in the drawing. Round the answer to whole centimeters.

   c. Find the length of BC. Are AC and BC about the same length in the drawing? In reality?

Nicole wants to draw a similar right triangle ABC with angle $B = 80°$.

   d. Explain why it is not possible to make this drawing in your notebook. What is the length of BC in this triangle? In reality?

   e. What is your conclusion about the lengths of AC and BC if the size of the glide angle increases?

Directions for painters state that a ladder is placed safely against a wall if the angle with the ground is about 70°. Consider a ladder that is 10 m long.

7. **a.** Make a drawing to scale of this ladder where it is placed safely against the wall. Show what you did to make the drawing.

   b. About how far from the wall is this 10-m ladder?

The Ratios: Tangent, Sine, Cosine

In right triangles, we have three sides: the hypotenuse (the ladder) and the legs of the right triangle (the height and distance) that help define the glide ratio.

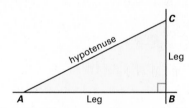

Reaching All Learners

Accommodation

Help students draw problem 6a by having them draw segment AB first, and then making angle B 40°.

Intervention

You may want to discuss how arrow strings and reverse arrow strings can be used to solve $\frac{AC}{5} = 0.839$:

$$AC \xrightarrow{\ \times 5\ } 0.893$$
$$\xleftarrow{\ \div 5\ }$$

Solutions and Samples

6. a.

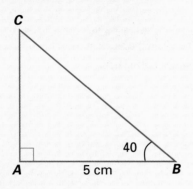

b. Tangent 40° ≈ 0.839.

$\frac{AC}{AB}$ ≈ 0.839; $\frac{AC}{5}$ ≈ 0.839; AC ≈ 5 × 0.839 = 4.195.

Side AC is in the drawing about 4 cm.

c. Using the Pythagorean theorem :

$BC^2 = AB^2 + AC^2$.

$BC^2 = 5^2 + 4^2 = 25 + 16 = 41$.

BC ≈ 6.4 cm.

In the drawing AC is about 4 cm; in reality it is about 4 × 200 = 800 m.

In the drawing BC is about 6.4 cm; in reality this is about 6.4 × 200 = 1,280 m.

BC is longer than AC both in the drawing and in reality. AC is about two thirds of BC.

d. The drawing does not fit on a notebook page; the hypotenuse and the longer leg do not meet.

tan 80° = 5.671

$\frac{AC}{AB}$ = 5.671; $\frac{AC}{5}$ = 5.671;

AC = 5 × 5.671 =

28.355 ≈ 28.4 cm

$BC^2 = AB^2 + AC^2$

$BC^2 = 5^2 + 28.355^2$ =

25 + 804 = 829

BC ≈ 28.792 cm ≈ 28.8 cm

In the drawing, BC is about 28.8 cm; in reality this is about 5,758 m.

e. As the size of the glide angle (B) increases, the length of sides AC and BC get closer.

Hints and Comments

Materials

Appendix A on Teacher's Guide pages 61A–62 (Student Book pages 68–70); calculator (one per student); protractor or compass card (one per student)

Overview

Students solve problems using the tangent ratio and the Pythagorean theorem. The text at the bottom of the page is an introduction to sine and cosine on the following page.

Planning

Students may work on problems 6 and 7 individually or in small groups. Discuss students' answers, as needed. Read the bottom of the page aloud in class.

7. a.

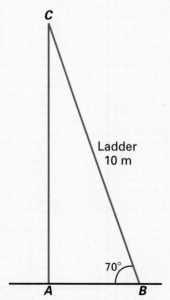

Answers will vary. Sample response:

First, I made a drawing of a 70° angle. For the ladder (BC) I marked off 10 cm (1 cm in the drawing stands for 1 m in reality). From that point I drew a line straight down to the ground (AC); this line represents the wall.

b. The ladder is about 3.5 m from the wall. Sample response:

I use the scale drawing I made in problem 7a. The distance between the ladder and the wall (AB) is about 3.5 cm. 1 cm stands for 1 m in reality, so AB is in reality 3.5 m.

Reasoning with Ratios

Notes

Read this page with students in class. Use the student drawing from problem 7 on the previous page to review this notation.

Point out to students that sine and cosine values are also included in Appendix A on Student Book pages 68–70.

In addition to the tangent ratio, there are two other ratios which describe a relationship between the sides of a right triangle.

One is the **sine ratio**, abbreviated sin α.

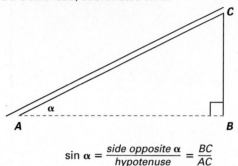

$$\sin \alpha = \frac{side\ opposite\ \alpha}{hypotenuse} = \frac{BC}{AC}$$

The other is the **cosine ratio**, abbreviated cos α.

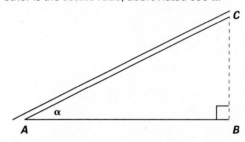

$$\cos \alpha = \frac{side\ adjacent\ to\ \alpha}{hypotenuse} = \frac{AB}{AC}$$

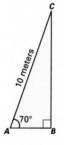

Notice that for both the sine and the cosine ratios, the hypotenuse is the "denominator."

Refer back to your scale drawing of the ladder situation in problem 7 where angle $A = 70°$ and the length of the ladder is 10 m.

$$\cos 70° = \frac{side\ adjacent\ to\ \alpha}{hypotenuse} = \frac{AB}{AC} = \frac{horizontal\ distance\ of\ the\ ladder\ to\ the\ wall}{length\ of\ the\ ladder}$$

Reaching All Learners

Vocabulary Building

The adjacent side is the side which helps form the angle, NOT the hypotenuse!

Intervention

Use the mnemonic, SOH-CAH-TOA, to help students remember the formulas:

SOH (**s**in = **o**pposite/**h**ypotenuse)

CAH (**c**os = **a**djacent/**h**ypotenuse)

TOA (**t**an = **o**pposite/**a**djacent)

Hints and Comments

Overview

In addition to the tangent ratio, on this page students learn about the sine and cosine ratio.

About the Mathematics

The concept of tangent is slowly and carefully built in this unit, eventually using the context of glide ratio as a model for the tangent concept. Formal notation is only introduced after careful concept building. The introduction of sine and cosine can now be very straightforward since the basic idea is the same. There are just other ratios that can be used, depending on what is known and what is needed (a particular side length or angle measure).

Notes

8 Draw and label the triangle to answer this question. Remind students that the length of the ladder is 10 m, as it says at the bottom of page 50 in problem 7.

9 Encourage students to make a drawing to answer these problems.

10–12 Remind students to refer to Appendix A on Student Book pages 68–70 to check their answers.

13a Remind students that the hypotenuse (ladder) is always the longest side.

8. a. Find the value of cos 70°. Use the table from the appendix or your calculator.

b. Use the cosine value to find the distance of the ladder to the wall. Show your calculation.

c. How high does this ladder reach on the wall? Use the sin 70° to make a calculation.

Answer the following questions. You can either use drawings, the table from the appendix, or your calculator.

9. Complete each ending.

If the angle is small,

a. the tangent ratio is …

b. the sine ratio is …

c. the cosine ratio is …

10. The tangent ratio can reach any positive value.

True or not true?

11. The sine ratio can reach any value.

True or not true?

12. The cosine ratio can never exceed 1.

True or not true?

A ladder is placed very steeply against a wall:

13. a. Explain why sin α is very close to 1 in this situation.

b. Explain why sin α is always smaller than 1.

c. Explain why tan α can be as large as you want.

Assessment Pyramid

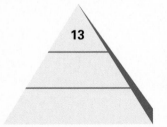

Solve problems using right triangle trigonometry ratios.

Reaching All Learners

Extension

For problems 9–12, have students prove their answers.

Intervention

Have students use pencils and a book to model the situations.

Solutions and Samples

8. a. cos 70° = 0.342

   b. cos 70° = $\dfrac{\text{distance of ladder to wall}}{\text{length of the ladder}}$

      0.342 = $\dfrac{\text{distance of ladder to wall}}{10}$

      10 × 0.342 = distance of ladder to wall = 3.42 m

   c. sin 70° = $\dfrac{\text{height reached on wall}}{\text{length of the ladder}}$

      0.940 = $\dfrac{\text{height reached on wall}}{10}$

      10 × 0.940 = height reached on wall = 9.4 m.

9.

If the angle is small,

   a. the tangent ratio is small.

   b. the sine ratio is small.

   c. the cosine ratio is close to 1.

10. True

11. Not true

12. True

13. Explanations may vary. Sample explanations:

   a. Angle α is very large and close to 90°, which makes the height just a little smaller than the length of the ladder. Since the sine ratio is the ratio of two nearly identical lengths, the ratio is close to 1. This means sin α is almost 1 too.

   b. The ladder (hypotenuse) will always be the longest side. The height can never exceed the length of the ladder.

   c. The tangent ratio is the ratio of the height reached on the wall to the horizontal distance. As the ladder moves closer to the wall and angle α gets larger and closer to 90°, tan α gets larger.

Hints and Comments

Materials

Appendix A on Teacher's Guide pages 61A–62 (Student Book pages 68–70); scientific calculator (one per student);

Overview

Students work on problems using tangent, sine, and cosine.

Planning

Students may work on problems 8–13 individually or in small groups. Discuss students' answers, as needed. In any case discuss students' answers to problems 8 and 9.

Comments About the Solutions

8. b. Refer back to problem 7b when discussing this problem.

You may ask students to reflect on both answers.

Sample response:

I get a more precise answer by calculating (3.42 m) than by using the scale drawing (about 3.5 m).

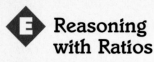
Notes

Glide angle, tangent of the glide angle, glide ratio, and slope are all measurements for the steepness of the flight path.

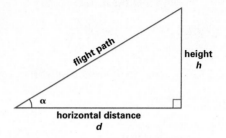

α = glide angle $\qquad$ $\tan \alpha = \frac{h}{d}$

glide ratio = $h{:}d$ or $\frac{h}{d}$ $\qquad$ slope = $h{:}d$ or $\frac{h}{d}$

This table compares several flight paths with varying degrees of steepness.

Flight Path	Height (in km)	Distance (in km)	Slope $(\frac{h}{d})$	α
1	6	11		
2		8	0.5	
3	4		$\frac{2}{5}$	
4		4.5		20°

14 Make sure students indicate the proper unit for their answers.

14a Students should write slopes as decimals and fractions. Make sure they have the correct answers before they do 14c.

14b When listing the flight paths in order from steepest to least steep, have students also list the angles so they see the correlation.

14. **a.** In your notebook, copy and complete the table.

   b. List the flight paths in order from the steepest to the least steep.

   c. Find the length of each flight path. Use the sine ratio, the cosine ratio, and the Pythagorean theorem at least one time each when you calculate the lengths.

Assessment Pyramid

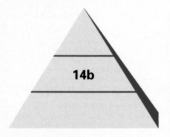

14b

Make relative comparisons involving steepness problems.

Reaching All Learners

Extension

Remind students to refer to their notes for the algorithms for sine, cosine, and tangent if necessary.

Intervention

Ask the students to sketch out and label triangles. Have them set up the tangent, sine, or cosine equations.

For problem 14c, you might want to offer a suggestion that they solve flight path 1 and 2 using the Pythagorean theorem, flight path 3 using sine, and flight path 4 using cosine.

Solutions and Samples

14. a.

Flight Path	Height (in km)	Distance (in km)	Slope $\left(\frac{h}{d}\right)$	α
1	6	11	$\frac{6}{11}$	29°
2	4	8	0.5	27°
3	4	10	$\frac{2}{5}$	22°
4	1.6	4.5	0.36	20°

Calculations:

Flight Path 1

$\tan \alpha = \frac{6}{11}$

$\alpha \approx 28.6°$ or 29°.

Flight Path 2

Ratio of height to distance is 0.5 or $\frac{1}{2}$.

When d is 8, then $h = 4$.

$\tan \alpha = 0.5$

$\alpha \approx 26.6°$ or 27°.

Flight Path 3

Ratio table:

Height	2	4
Distance	5	10

$\tan \alpha = \frac{2}{5}$

$\alpha \approx 21.8°$ or 22°.

Flight Path 4

$\tan 20° = \frac{h}{4.5}$.

$0.364 = \frac{h}{4.5}$

$h = 0.364 \times 4.5$

$h \approx 1.64$ or 1.6

Slope $= \frac{h}{d} = \frac{1.6}{4.5} \approx 0.36$.

b. Steepest: flight path 1.

then: flight path 2

then: flight path 3

Least steep: flight path 4

c. Flight Path 2 is about 8.9 or 9 km.

Using the Pythagorean Theorem:

Flight path is p.

$p^2 = 4^2 + 8^2$

$p = \sqrt{80} \approx 8.9$ or 9

Flight Path 3 is about 10.8 or 11 km.

Using the Pythagorean Theorem:

$p^2 = 4^2 + 10^2$

$p = \sqrt{116} \approx 10.8$ or 11

Hints and Comments

Overview

Students review the different measures for steepness they have learned about in this unit. They apply the tangent concept as well as the concepts of sine, cosine, and the Pythagorean theorem to complete a table with flight paths of varying steepness.

About the Mathematics

Note that at the top of this page the term slope is also used as a measure of steepness. Students should understand that slope is the same as the ratio of the height to the distance, or the glide ratio, or the tangent ratio they learned about in this unit. Slope is also used in the unit *Graphing Equations*. The term *slope* is also used in the table students will complete in problem 14. Students may think of slope as being the same as glide ratio.

Planning

Read the top of the page in class, paying attention to the use of the term *slope*. Students may work on problem 14 individually. You may want to discuss students' answers in class.

Comments About the Solutions

14. a. In order to compare the slopes of the different flight paths, it would be best to convert the ratios and fractions to decimals. You may want to refer to page 36 for that matter.

   b. Encourage students to explain their reasoning. Students by now should understand that the larger the angle (or the larger the slope), the steeper the flight path.

   c. Students may round off their answers.

Flight Path 1 is about 12 km.

Using the sine ratio:

$\sin 29° = \frac{h}{p} = 0.485$

$\frac{6}{p} = 0.485$

So $0.485p = 6$

$p = \frac{6}{0.485} \approx 12.4$ or about 12

Flight Path 4 is about 4.9, or 5 km.

Using the cosine ratio:

$\cos 20° = \frac{d}{p} = 0.94$

$\frac{4.5}{p} = 0.94$

So $0.94p = 4.5$

$p = \frac{4.5}{0.94} \approx 4.8$

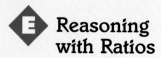
 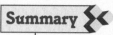 **Reasoning with Ratios**

Summary ➤◄

In this unit, many different situations play a role—vision lines, shadows and light rays, steepness of ladders, glide paths, glide angle, and glide ratios. All situations involve a right triangle, which plays a vital role.

The steepness of a ladder and the glide ratio can be expressed with the mathematical ratio called the tangent ratio.

Right triangles were explored somewhat further.

- You made use of the Pythagorean theorem to find an unknown side's length.
- You investigated two new ratios, the sine ratio and cosine ratio.

Check Your Work ➤

A pole 7 m long is placed against a wall at an angle of 45°.

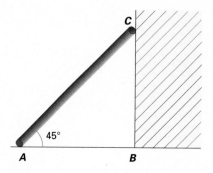

1. How high is *BC*?

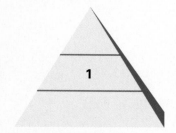
Reaching All Learners

Advanced Learners

Encourage students to further investigate the relationship between the sine and cosine ratios by finding angle pairs for which the ratios for sine and cosine are equal. For example,

sin 30	cos 60
sin 90	cos 0
sin 10	cos 80
sin 25	cos 65

Have students find other angle pairs and encourage students to develop an explanation of why these angle pairs for sine and cosine have the same ratio.

Solutions and Samples

Answers to Check Your Work

1. $BC \approx 4.9$, or 5.

   Calculation:

   $$\sin 45° = \frac{BC}{7}$$
   $$0.707 = \frac{BC}{7}$$
   $$0.707 \times 7 = BC$$
   $$BC = 4.949 \approx 4.9, \text{ or } 5$$

Hints and Comments

Overview

Students read the Summary, which reviews the main concepts covered in this section. Students use the Check Your Work problems as self-assessment. The answers to these problems are also provided on Student Book page 67.

After students complete Section E, you may assign as homework appropriate activities from the Additional Practice section, located on Student Book page 60. After students have completed Section E, you may use the Unit Test with students as a culminating assessment.

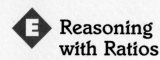
Notes

Students may round off
their answers as long as
they indicate that the
answers are approximations.

A roof is constructed according to this diagram:

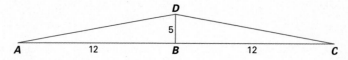

2. a. How long should *AD* and *DC* be?

   b. How large is angle *A*?

The road *AC* is 10 km long and angle *A* = 10°.

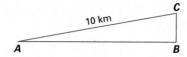

3. What is height *BC* at the end of the road?

For Further Reflection

Make sure students'
drawings are properly
labeled. You may want to
encourage them to use
letter labels of the sides for
their overview.

For Further Reflection

Make a drawing of a right triangle, labeled △*PQR*. The angle
measurement of ∠*Q* = 90°.

Make an overview of the side ratios—sine, cosine, and tangent—
for this triangle.

Assessment Pyramid

2, 3, ◼FFR

Assesses Section E Goals

Reaching All Learners

Intervention

Students may want to turn back to the pages describing the sine, cosine,
and tangent ratios.

Solutions and Samples

2. a. $AC = BC = 13$.

Calculation, using the Pythagorean theorem:

$AD^2 = 5^2 + 12^2$

$AD^2 = 25 + 144$

$AD^2 = 169$

$AD = \sqrt{169} = 13$

And since $AC = BC$, BC is also 13.

b. 23°.

Calculation:

$\tan \angle A = \frac{5}{12}$

So $\angle A = 22.6°$, or 23°.

3. $BC = 1.74$, or 2.

Calculation:

$\sin 10° = \frac{BC}{10}$

$0.174 = \frac{BC}{10}$

$10 \times 0.174 = BC$

$BC = 1.74$, or 2

For Further Reflection

Sample response:

$\sin \angle R = \frac{PQ}{PR}$.

$\cos \angle R = \frac{RQ}{PR}$.

$\tan \angle R = \frac{PQ}{RQ}$.

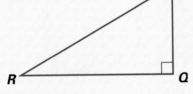

Overview

Students continue using the Check Your Work problems as self-assessment.

Additional Practice

Section Ⓐ Now You See It, Now You Don't

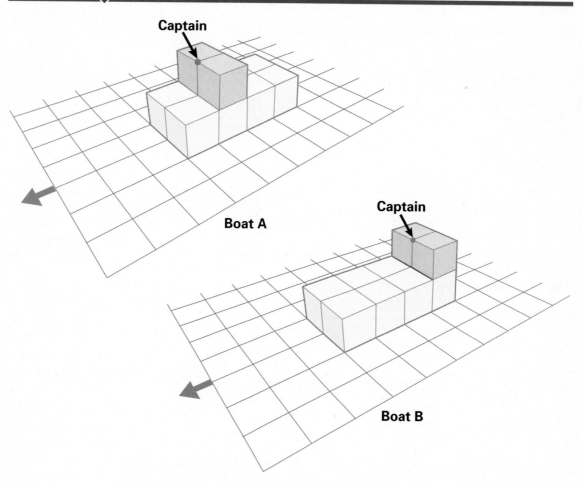

Captain

Boat A

Captain

Boat B

The drawings show two boat models made with 1-cm blocks. Imagine that the boats are sailing in the direction shown by the arrows.

1. On graph paper or **Student Activity Sheet 2**, make side-view and top-view drawings of each boat.

2. On your drawings, include vision lines for the captain, who can look straight ahead and sideways, and shade in the blind area.

3. How many square units is the blind area of boat A? boat B?

4. On your side-view drawings of each boat, measure and label the angle between the water and the vision line.

5. On which boat is the captain's view the best? Explain.

Section A. Now You See It, Now You Don't

1. and **2.**

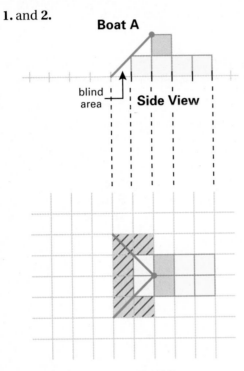

Top View

Top View

3. The blind area of Boat A is 6 square units. The blind area of Boat B is 18 square units.

4. The angle between the water and the vision line is 45° for Boat A and about 18° for Boat B.

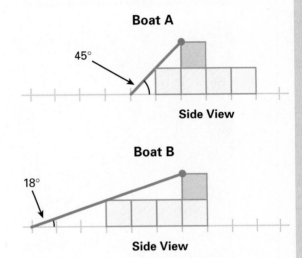

5. The captain of Boat A has a better view. Explanations will vary. Sample explanations:

The captain whose boat has the smallest blind area will have the best view. Boat A's blind area is smaller (6 square units) than Boat B's blind area (18 square units). Therefore, the captain of Boat A has a better view.

The angle between the water and the vision line for Boat A is larger (45°) than the angle for Boat B (18°). Boat A has a vision line that is steeper, so its blind area is smaller, and its captain has a better view.

Section **B** Shadows and Blind Spots

The height of a pyramid can be determined by studying the shadows caused by the sun.

Suppose that you put a stick into the ground near a pyramid. As shown in the drawing, the length of the stick above ground is 1 m, and its shadow caused by the sun is 1.5 m long.

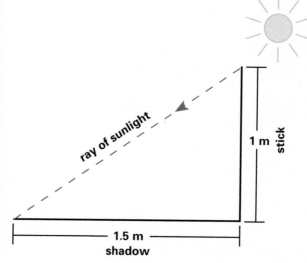

ray of sunlight

1 m
stick

1.5 m
shadow

1. a. If the shadow of the pyramid is pointing northeast, what direction is the shadow of the stick pointing?

   b. From what direction is the sun shining?

The picture to the left shows the pyramid and its shadow at the same time of day. The length of the pyramid's shadow, measured from the center of the pyramid, is 240 m.

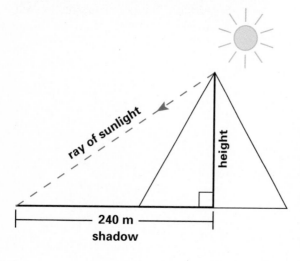

ray of sunlight

height

240 m
shadow

2. Compare the height of the stick and the length of its shadow to find the height of the pyramid. Explain your reasoning.

Section B. Shadows and Blind Spots

1. a. The stick's shadow is pointing in the same direction as the pyramid's shadow—northeast.

b. The sun is shining from the opposite direction—southwest. Shadows produced by the sun point in the direction opposite the position of the sun in the sky.

2. The pyramid is 160 meters high. Explanations will vary. Sample explanations:

- The length of the stick's shadow is 1.5 times the stick's height. Similarly, the length of the pyramid's shadow will be 1.5 times the pyramid's height. Since the pyramid's shadow is 240 meters long, dividing 240 meters by 1.5 gives the height of the pyramid: $240 \div 1.5 = 160$. So the pyramid is 160 meters high.

- There is a fixed ratio between the height of an object and the length of its shadow at a certain moment in time. Using a ratio table and a height of 160 meters:

Object Height (in m)	1	2	160
Shadow Length (in m)	1.5	3	240

$\times 2$ $\times 80$

- Using language:

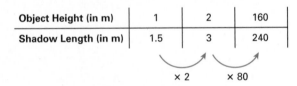

For the pyramid the length of the shadow is 240 m. So 240:1.5 gives the height of the pyramid, which is 160 m.

Additional Practice

Section ⟨C⟩ Shadows and Angles

1. Use a compass card or a protractor and a ruler to make side-view drawings to scale of the following ladders. Each ladder is leaning against a wall.

   Ladder A

   • The distance between the foot of the ladder and the wall is 3 m.

   • The angle between the ladder and the ground is 60°.

   Ladder B

   • The distance between the foot of the ladder and the wall is 4 m.

   • The ladder touches the wall at a height of 6 m.

2. Determine the height-to-distance ratio for each ladder.

3. What is the angle between ladder B and the ground?

4. Which ladder is steeper, ladder A or ladder B? Explain.

Section ⟨D⟩ Glide Angles

Use your calculator or the table in the appendix to solve the following problems.

1. **a.** If $\tan A = \frac{1}{20}$, what is the measurement of $\angle A$?

   b. If $\tan B = 20$, what is the measurement of $\angle B$?

Marco is comparing two hang gliders. He takes one test flight with each glider from a cliff that is 50 m high. The following picture shows the path for each flight. Note: The picture is not drawn to scale.

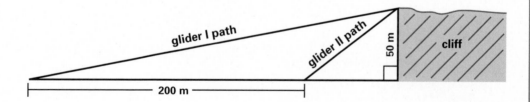

Section C. Shadows and Angles

1. In the sample drawings below, one centimeter represents one meter.

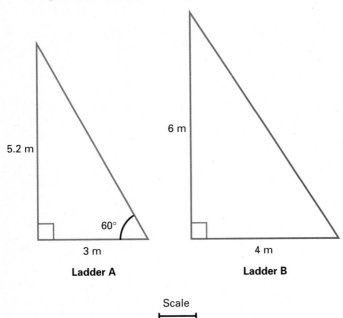

Ladder A

Ladder B

Scale
|———|
1 m

2. Ladder A 5.2:3 = 1.7:1 = 1:0.6 = 1.7

Ladder B 6:4 = 1.5:1 = 1:0.7 = 1.5

In order to find the height-to-distance ratio for Ladder A, students need to measure the height of the wall in their scale drawings.

3. About 56°

4. Ladder A is steeper than Ladder B. Explanations will vary. Sample explanation:

The steeper ladder will have a larger angle between its foot and the ground. Since the angle between the foot of the ladder and the ground is larger for Ladder A (60°) than it is for Ladder B (56°), Ladder A is steeper than Ladder B.

Section D: Glide Angles

1. a. About 3°

b. About 87°

(Note: Tan A and tan B have opposite $h{:}d$ ratios, $\frac{1}{20}$ and 20. That means that the sum of their angles, 3° + 87°, must be 90°. However, due to rounding, students may not get exactly 90 degrees.)

The glide ratio of glider I is 1:20, and glider I travels 200 m farther than glider II.

2. What is the glide ratio of glider II?

3. In the picture below, the measurement of $\angle D$ is 45° and the measurement of $\angle A$ is 30°. If the length of side BD is 10 cm, how long is side AB?

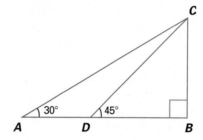

The following picture shows two cliffs that are 100 m apart. One cliff is 20 m high and the other is 30 m high. Imagine that a hang glider takes off from the top of each cliff. The two hang gliders have the same glide ratio and land at the same location.

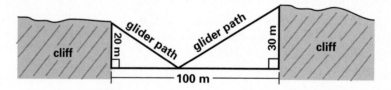

4. How far from each cliff do the gliders land?

5. Suppose that a glider has a glide ratio of 5%.

   a. What do you think a glide ratio of 5% means?

   b. What is the glide angle for this glider?

2. The glide ratio for glider II is 1:16. Since the glide ratio of glider I is 1:20, glider I must travel a distance that is 20 times the height of the cliff; 20 × 50 meters = 1,000 meters. The difference between the distance traveled by glider I and that traveled by glider II is 200 m, so glider II travels 1,000 m − 200 m = 800 m. Therefore, glider II has a glide ratio of 50:800 or 5:80, or 1:16.

3. Side *AB* is about 17.3 cm long. The tangent of angle *D* is tan 45° = 1, so the height-to-distance ratio of side *CB* to side *DB* is 1:1. Since side *DB* is 10 cm long, that means the length of side *CB* is also 10 cm (10:10 is the same ratio as 1:1). Using the tangent table in Appendix A, you can find that tan 30° = 0.577, so the height-to-distance ratio of side *CB* to side *AB* can be found by using a calculator and the following ratio table:

	× 1,000	÷ 57.7	
Height of Side *CB* (in cm)	0.577	577	10
Distance of Side *AB* (in cm)	1	1,000	17.3

4. The 30-meter cliff is 1.5 times higher than the 20-meter cliff (20 m × 1.5 = 30 m). Because the two gliders have the same glide ratio, the glider launched from the 30-meter cliff will travel a distance that is 1.5 times farther than the distance traveled by the glider launched from the 20-meter cliff.

To find the location where the gliders land, divide the distance between the two cliffs (100 m) into two parts that are in the ratio 1:1.5. The ratio 1:1.5 is equal to 2:3 = 4:6 = 40:60. Because 40 + 60 = 100, the glider on the left has to land 40 meters from the left cliff, and the glider on the right has to land 60 meters from the right cliff.

5. a. Answers will vary. Sample response:

A 5% glide ratio means that the hang glider has a height to distance ratio of 5:100, or 1:20.

b. About 3°. The glide angle α for a glider with a glide ratio of 1:20 is tan α = $\frac{1}{20}$ = 0.05. Using Appendix A, students can find that α is equal to about 3°.

Additional Practice

Section **E** Reasoning with Ratios

1. Make a drawing of a right triangle with an angle of 45°. Use this drawing to show that sin 45° = cos 45°.

2. Use the drawing from problem 1. Sides *AB* and *BC* are 1.

   Use the Pythagorean theorem to find the value of sin 45°.

3. Complete the following table:

α	sin α	cos α
10°		
20°		
30°		
40°		
50°		
60°		
70°		
80°		

4. Explain the results of the table by comparing the values for sine and cosine.

Section E. Reasoning with Ratios

1.

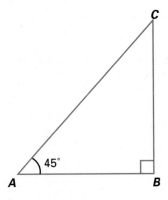

$\sin \angle A = \frac{BC}{AC}$

$\cos \angle A = \frac{AB}{AC}$

But since $\angle A = 45°$: $AB = BC$ and, therefore, $\sin \angle A = \cos \angle A$.

2. $AB^2 + BC^2 = AC^2$

$\qquad 1 + 1 = AC^2$

$\qquad\qquad AC = \sqrt{2} \approx 1.4$

$\sin 45° \approx \frac{1}{1.4} \approx 0.7$

3.

α	sin α	cos α
10°	0.174	0.985
20°	0.342	0.940
30°	0.5	0.866
40°	0.643	0.766
50°	0.766	0.643
60°	0.866	0.5
70°	0.940	0.342
80°	0.985	0.174

4. Sample response:

I noticed that sin 10° = cos 80°, and sin 20° = cos 70°, so when two angles are together 90°, the sine of one angle equals the cosine of the other.

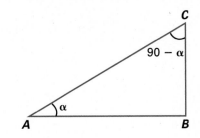

$\sin \alpha = \frac{BC}{AC} = \cos(90 - \alpha)$

Appendices

Appendix A

Angle Degree	Sine	Cosine	Tangent
0°	0.000	1.00	0.000
1°	0.017	1.00	0.017
2°	0.035	0.999	0.035
3°	0.052	0.999	0.052
4°	0.070	0.998	0.070
5°	0.087	0.996	0.087
6°	0.105	0.995	0.105
7°	0.122	0.993	0.123
8°	0.139	0.990	0.141
9°	0.156	0.988	0.158
10°	0.174	0.985	0.176
11°	0.191	0.982	0.194
12°	0.208	0.978	0.213
13°	0.225	0.974	0.231
14°	0.242	0.970	0.249
15°	0.259	0.966	0.268
16°	0.276	0.961	0.287
17°	0.292	0.956	0.306
18°	0.309	0.951	0.325
19°	0.326	0.946	0.344
20°	0.342	0.940	0.360
21°	0.358	0.934	0.384
22°	0.375	0.927	0.404
23°	0.391	0.921	0.424
24°	0.407	0.914	0.445
25°	0.423	0.906	0.466
26°	0.438	0.899	0.488
27°	0.454	0.891	0.510
28°	0.469	0.883	0.532
29°	0.485	0.875	0.554
30°	0.500	0.866	0.577

Appendix A

Angle Degree	Sine	Cosine	Tangent
31°	0.515	0.857	0.601
32°	0.530	0.848	0.625
33°	0.545	0.839	0.649
34°	0.559	0.829	0.675
35°	0.574	0.819	0.700
36°	0.588	0.809	0.727
37°	0.602	0.799	0.754
38°	0.616	0.788	0.781
39°	0.629	0.777	0.810
40°	0.643	0.766	0.839
41°	0.656	0.755	0.869
42°	0.669	0.743	0.900
43°	0.682	0.731	0.933
44°	0.695	0.719	0.966
45°	0.707	0.707	1.000
46°	0.719	0.695	1.036
47°	0.731	0.682	1.072
48°	0.743	0.669	1.111
49°	0.755	0.656	1.150
50°	0.766	0.643	1.192
51°	0.777	0.629	1.235
52°	0.788	0.616	1.280
53°	0.799	0.602	1.327
54°	0.809	0.588	1.376
55°	0.819	0.574	1.428
56°	0.829	0.559	1.483
57°	0.839	0.545	1.540
58°	0.848	0.530	1.600
59°	0.857	0.515	1.664
60°	0.866	0.500	1.732
61°	0.875	0.485	1.804

Appendix A

Angle Degree	Sine	Cosine	Tangent
62°	0.883	0.469	1.881
63°	0.891	0.454	1.963
64°	0.899	0.438	2.050
65°	0.906	0.423	2.145
66°	0.914	0.407	2.246
67°	0.921	0.391	2.356
68°	0.927	0.375	2.475
69°	0.934	0.358	2.605
70°	0.940	0.342	2.748
71°	0.946	0.326	2.904
72°	0.951	0.309	3.078
73°	0.956	0.292	3.271
74°	0.961	0.276	3.487
75°	0.966	0.259	3.732
76°	0.970	0.242	4.011
77°	0.974	0.225	4.332
78°	0.978	0.208	4.705
79°	0.982	0.191	5.145
80°	0.985	0.174	5.671
81°	0.988	0.156	6.314
82°	0.990	0.139	7.115
83°	0.993	0.122	8.144
84°	0.995	0.105	9.514
85°	0.996	0.087	11.43
86°	0.998	0.070	14.30
87°	0.999	0.052	19.08
88°	0.999	0.035	28.64
89°	1.00	0.017	57.29
90°	1.00	0.000	

BRITANNICA

Mathematics
in
Context

Assessment

Assessment Overview

Unit assessments in *Mathematics in Context* include two quizzes and a Unit Test. Quiz 1 is to be used anytime after students have completed Section B. Quiz 2 can be used after students have completed Section D. The Unit Test addresses most of the major goals of the unit. You can evaluate student responses to these assessments to determine what each student knows about the content goals addressed in this unit.

Pacing

Each quiz is designed to take approximately 25 minutes to complete. The unit test is designed to be completed during a 45-minute class period. For more information on how to use these assessments, see the Planning Assessment section on the next page.

Goals	Assessment Opportunities	Problem Levels
• Understand the concepts of vision line, angle, and blind spot.	Quiz 1 Problems 1b, 2ab Test Problems 1, 2, 5	
• Understand the concept of glide ratio or tangent.	Quiz 2 Problems 1, 3	
• Construct and measure vision lines and blind spots (or light rays and shadows) in two- and three-dimensional representations.	Quiz 1 Problems 1b, 2ab Test Problems 3, 5	I
• Measure angles.	Quiz 1 Problems 1a, 3 Test Problem 8	
• Make scale drawings of situations.	Quiz 2 Problem 3 Test Problem 12	
• Make relative comparisons involving steepness problems.	Quiz 2 Problem 2	
• Understand the relationship among steepness, angle, and height-to-distance ratio.	Test Problems 9, 11, 12, 13	II
• Understand the ratio between an object and its shadow caused by the sun for different times of the year.	Test Problems 6, 7	
• Use ratios to solve problems.	Test Problems 4, 10	
• Solve problems using right triangle trigonometry ratios.	Test Problems 9, 10, 13	III

About the Mathematics

These assessment activities assess the majority of the goals for *Looking at an Angle.* Refer to the Goals and Assessment Opportunities sections on the previous page for information regarding the goals that are assessed in each problem. Some of the problems that involve multiple skills and processes address more than one unit goal. To assess students' ability to engage in non-routine problem solving (a Level III goal in the Assessment Pyramid), some problems assess students' ability to use their skills and conceptual knowledge in new situations. For example, in Theresa's blind spot problem on the Unit Test (Problem 4), students must use ratios and a map scale to decide whether or not the time a friend walks through a blind area is reasonable.

Planning Assessment

These assessments are designed for individual assessment, however some problems can be done in pairs or small groups. It is important that students work individually if you want to evaluate each student's understanding and abilities.

Make sure you allow enough time for students to complete the problems. If students need more than one class session to complete the problems, it is suggested that they finish during the next mathematics class or you may assign select problems as a take-home activity. Students should be free to solve the problems their own way. Calculators may be used on the quizzes or Unit Test if students choose to use them.

If individual students have difficulties with any particular problems, you may give the student the option of making a second attempt after providing him/her a hint. You may also decide to use one of the optional problems or Extension activities not previously done in class as additional assessments for students who need additional help.

Scoring

Solution and scoring guides are included for each quiz and the Unit Test. The method of scoring depends on the types of questions on each assessment. A holistic scoring approach could also be used to evaluate an entire quiz.

Several problems require students to explain their reasoning or justify their answers. For these questions, the reasoning used by students in solving the problems as well as the correctness of the answers, should be considered in your scoring and grading scheme.

Student progress toward goals of the unit should be considered when reviewing student work. Descriptive statements and specific feedback are often more informative to students than a total score or grade. You might choose to record descriptive statements of select aspects of student work as evidence of student progress toward specific goals of the unit that you have identified as essential.

Looking at an Angle Quiz 1

Use additional paper as needed.

1. The picture below shows a cross section of a canyon.

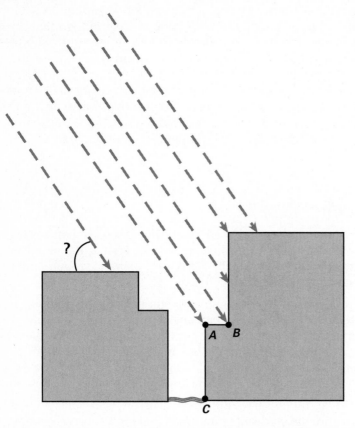

The picture shows that in the morning ledge *AB* lies in the sun.

a. Measure the angle between the sun's rays and the horizon.
   (The angle is indicated in the picture with **?**).

A while later, the sun's rays have just reached *C*, but the river below is still in the shadow.

b. Make a drawing representing this situation.

© Encyclopædia Britannica, Inc. This page may be reproduced for classroom use.

2.

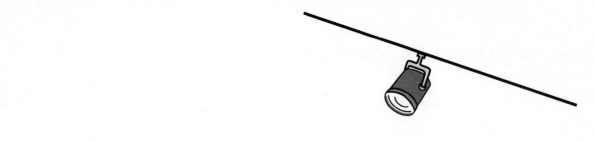

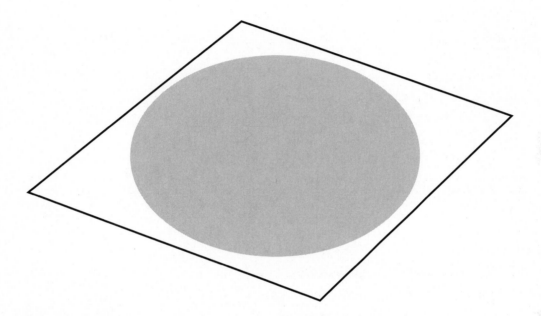

This is a picture of a lamp casting a shadow of a ball on the ground. The ball was deleted from the picture.

a. In the picture above, draw two possible positions for the ball.

b. Is it possible to get this shadow if the ball is lying on the ground? Explain.

Use additional paper as needed.

1. The picture below shows a cross section of a canyon.

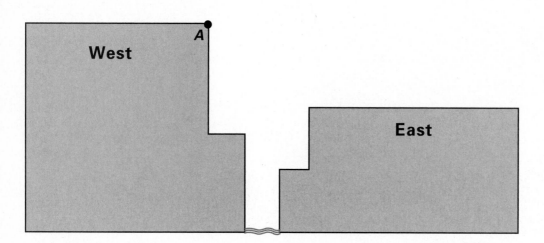

- The drawing is not to scale.
- The east rim is 100 meters lower than the west rim.
- A glider flies above point A, 50 meters above the rim.
- The canyon rims are, horizontally, 2 kilometers apart.

Can the glider with a glide ratio of 1:22 safely reach the east rim?
Show your work.

Mathematics in Context

2. Excellent high-tech sail planes have a glide ratio better than 1:40. What is the glide angle of these sail planes and the tangent of the glide angle?

3. For a ladder to be considered safe, it is important that the tangent of the angle between the ladder and the floor is between 3 and 4. What angle measures between the ladder and the floor are safe?

Looking at an Angle Unit Test

Use additional paper as needed.

Investigating the Mammoth Rocks

Two scientists, Jorge and Theresa, are studying in the southwestern part of the United States. They are investigating rock formations, deserts, plants, and animals. They are an adventurous pair—hiking in canyons, climbing rocks, and hang gliding are some of their favorite ways to explore and investigate. Today they are working in Mammoth Rock Country.

Shown below is a map of the area where they are working.

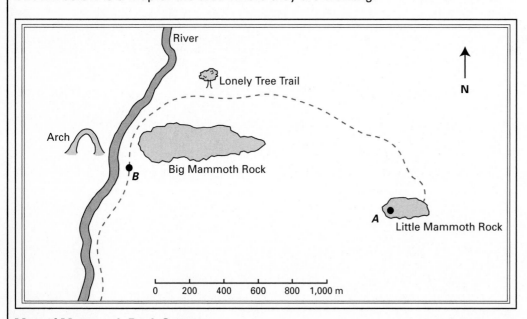

Map of Mammoth Rock Country

Mathematics in Context

Shown below is a picture that was taken in Mammoth Rock Country.

1. Find a location on the map where the photographer may have been standing while taking this picture. Mark the spot with an "X" on the map on the previous page.

Jorge and Theresa have just climbed Little Mammoth Rock. Theresa is at point A, about to take a hang glider flight. However, she will only start the flight when Jorge has descended the rock and has arrived at point B. Jorge is following the trail as he hikes. Theresa watches him from where she is sitting at point A. After a while, near Lonely Tree, Jorge disappears behind Big Mammoth Rock. Theresa waits and waits, but Jorge seems to stay out of sight forever. He has been in the "blind area" for half an hour.

2. Outline the blind area behind the rock on the map on the previous page.

3. How long is the part of the trail in that blind area? Make an estimate using the scale line.

Use additional paper as needed.

Under normal circumstances, a person can walk about 2 or 3 kilometers per hour.

4. Is there a reason for Theresa to be worried? Explain your answer.

As Theresa waits for Jorge to reappear, she wonders if he is walking in the shadow of the rock or in the sun. She notices that the shadow of Little Mammoth Rock just reaches the bottom of Big Mammoth Rock. Theresa knows that Little Mammoth Rock is twice the height of Big Mammoth Rock. She draws the shadow on the map. It looks like this:

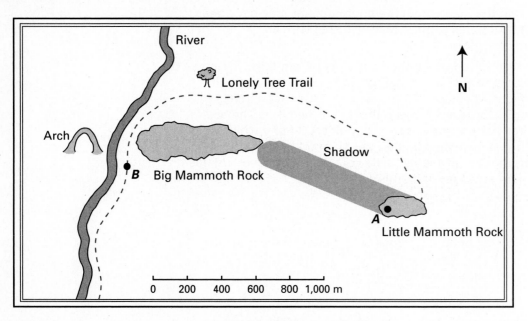

5. Draw the shadow of Big Mammoth Rock in the picture above.
Be precise in drawing the shadow's length and direction.

Below you see three top-view drawings of the arch and its shadow at different times on one day.

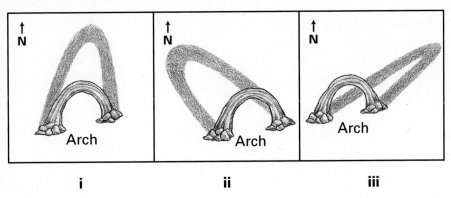

6. In which order were these drawings made?

7. Draw the shadow of the arch at sunset in the picture below.
   Be precise in drawing the shadow's length and direction.
   Explain why you drew the shadow that way.

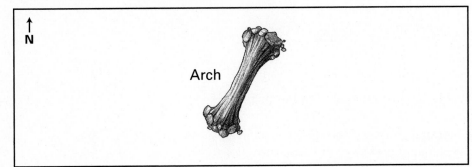

Use additional paper as needed.

Below is a sketch of a side view of the two rocks. The line represents the sun's ray. The distance between the two rocks is 910 meters.

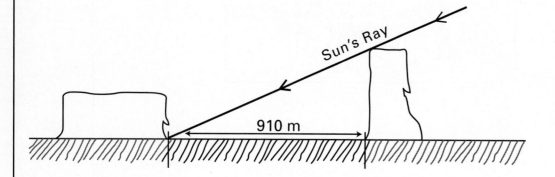

Sun's Ray

910 m

8. Measure the angle between the sun's ray and the horizon with a compass card or protractor.

9. Compute the height of Little Mammoth Rock. Show your work.

Hours later, the rock's shadow is six times longer than the height of the rock.

10. Compute the angle between the sun's ray and the horizon in this situation. Write an explanation of how you found the answer. Show your work.

Mathematics in Context

Finally, Jorge reappears behind Big Mammoth Rock. He uses his walkie-talkie to tell Theresa that an injured hiker has been calling for help. The hiker is on the other side of the river near the arch (see the map). He asks Theresa to fly in her hang glider across the river to the hiker in order to help him. Theresa tells Jorge that she is not sure she can reach that spot. Her hang glider has a glide ratio of 1:6.5.

11. Can Theresa reach the wounded hiker with her hang glider from Little Mammoth Rock? Show your work.

(Note: to solve this problem you need the height of the Little Mammoth Rock you calculated in problem 9. If you haven't found an answer for problem 9, you can use for problem 11 a height of 350 meters.)

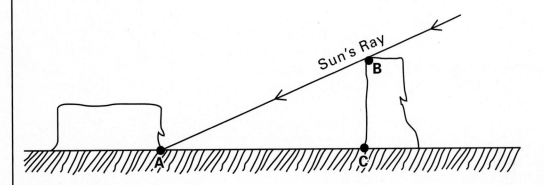

The distance between Big Mammoth Rock and Little Mammoth Rock (*AC*) is 910 m. For the height of the Little Mammoth Rock you can use your answer from problem 9, or you can use a height of 350 meters.

12. Find the length of *AB* using the Pythagorean theorem. Show your work.

13. Find the length of *AB* using sine or cosine. Show your work.

Looking at an Angle Quiz 1
Solution and Scoring Guide

Possible student answer	Suggested number of score points	Problem level
1. a. The angle is about 55°.	2	I
b.	3	I
2. a. Student answers may vary. See example:	3 (Award 1 score point for each correct position of the ball, 1 score point for accuracy of the drawing.)	I
b. Yes. See drawing:	2	I
Total score points	10	

Possible student answer	Suggested number of score points	Problem level
1. Student answers may vary. See example: **50 m** **West** **150 m** **100 m** **2,000 m** **East** This sketch shows that the glider is at a point 150 m higher than the point it needs to reach. It needs to cover a horizontal distance of 2,000 m. The glider has a glide ratio of 1:22. This means that for every meter height it can cover 22 m distance. From a height of 150 m, it can cover a distance of 22 × 150 m = 3,300 m. It needs to cover only 2,000 m. So the glider can easily reach the east rim. (Students could also include the following: Since the ratio 150:2,000 > 1:22, the glider can safely reach the east rim.)	**4** (Award 3 points for a correct explanation, 1 point for a correct conclusion.)	I
2. Answers may vary. Example: The glide ratio is better than 1:40 or, as a decimal, 0.025. The tangent table shows that an angle between 1° and 2° (say 1.5°) would give a tangent of 0.025. If the glide ratio should be better than 1:40, this means that the glide angle should be smaller than 1.5° and the tangent should be smaller than 0.025. The smaller the glide angle, the smaller the tangent and the better the glide ratio.	**3**	II
3. A safe angle for the ladder is between 72° and 75°. Answers may vary. Example: The tangent table shows that: an angle of 71° gives a tangent of 2.904; an angle of 72° gives a tangent of 3.078. This means that the angle should be no smaller than 72°. The tangent table also shows that: an angle of 75° gives a tangent of 3.732; an angle of 76° gives a tangent of 4.011. This means that the angle should be no bigger than 75°.	**3**	I
Total score points	**10**	

Looking at an Angle Unit Test
Solution and Scoring Guide

Possible student answer	Suggested number of score points	Problem level
1. Answers will vary. Sample response: *[map showing X, Lonely Tree Trail, Arch, B, Big Mammoth Rock, A, Little Mammoth Rock, N compass, scale 0 200 400 600 800 1,000 m]*	1	I
2. *[map showing River, Lonely Tree Trail, Arch, B, Big Mammoth Rock, A, Little Mammoth Rock, N compass, vision lines, scale 0 200 400 600 800 1,000 m]*	2 (Award 1 point for each correct vision line.)	I
3. Answers will vary. Accept estimates from 500–600 meters.	1	I
4. Answers and explanations will vary. Sample explanation: Walking at 2 kilometers an hour means that a person can walk 1 kilometer in half an hour. Since that section of the trail is closer to $\frac{1}{2}$ kilometer than to 1 kilometer, Theresa should begin to worry because he can walk that distance in about 15 minutes. However, waiting 15 minutes may feel like a very long time.	2 (Award 1 point for a correct explanation, 1 point for a correct conclusion.)	III

Possible student answer	Suggested number of score points	Problem level
5. ![Map showing River, Lonely Tree Trail, Arch, B Big Mammoth Rock, Shadow, A Little Mammoth Rock, with scale 0 200 400 600 800 1,000 m and N arrow] Since Little Mammoth Rock is twice as tall as Big Mammoth Rock, its shadow must be twice as long. Little Mammoth Rock's shadow measures about 3.6 cm on the student page, so Big Mammoth Rock's shadow should be about 1.8 cm long. The shadow of Big Mammoth Rock should point in the same direction as the shadow of Little Mammoth Rock.	2 (Award 1 point for each correct shadow. An explanation is not necessary.)	I
6. The correct order of the pictures is **ii, i, iii**. Explanations will vary. Sample explanation: In picture **i**, the sun is shining from the south; in picture **ii**, it is shining from the southeast; and in picture , it is shining from the southwest. Since the sun rises in the east and sets in the west, the correct order of the pictures is **ii, i, iii**.	2	II
7. ![Image of Arch with long shadow and N arrow] The sun sets in the west. At sunset, the shadow of the arch will be very long and will point to the east.	2 (Award 1 point for a correct answer, 1 point for a correct explanation.)	II
8. The angle is 23°. (Note: Accept 22°, 23°, or 24°)	2	I

Looking at an Angle Unit Test
Solution and Scoring Guide

Possible student answer	Suggested number of score points	Problem level
9. 386 meters The angle of the sun's ray is 23°. The tangent of 23° is equal to the height of the rock divided by the length of its shadow: tan of 23° = 0.424 = $\frac{h}{910}$ m h = 0.424 × 910 m = 386 meters Note: If the angle was measured at 22°, then the height is 368 meters. If the angle was measured at 24°, then the height is 405 meters.	**2** (Award 1 point for a correct answer, 1 point for correct student work.)	**II/III**
10. The angle between the sun's ray and the ground is about 9.5°. Some students may reason that since the shadow is six times longer than the height of the rock, the ratio of the height to the length of the shadow is $h{:}d$ = 1:6, or 0.167. Using the tangent table or calculator, students should find that a tangent of 0.167 corresponds to an angle of between 9° and 10°. h = 386 d = 6 × 386 = 2,316 so 386 ÷ 2,316 = 0.167	**3** (Award 1 point for a correct estimate, 2 points for a correct explanation.)	**III**
11. Yes. Strategies will vary. Sample strategy: From Little Mammoth Rock to the arch is approximately 1,800 meters. Theresa may use a ratio table to find out whether she can reach the injured hiker. The ratio table shows that if Theresa launches her glider from a height of 300 meters, she can go 1,950 meters. Since Little Mammoth is 386 meters high, she will make it.	**3** (Award 1 point for a correct answer, 2 points for a correct explanation.)	**II**

For problem 11, the ratio table:

	× 10	× 10	× 2	+ column 3
Height (in m)	1	10	100	200	300
Distance (in m)	6.5	65	650	1,300	1,950

Possible student answer	Suggested number of score points	Problem level
12. $910^2 + 386^2 = AB^2$ $828,100 + 148,996 = AB^2$ $977096 = AB^2$ $AB \approx 988$ m Using 350 m as height: $9102 + 3502 = AB^2$ $828,100 + 122,500 = AB^2$ $950,600 = AB^2$ $AB \approx 975$ m	**3** (Award 1 point for a correct answer, 2 points for correct student work.)	I/II
13. $\angle A = 23°$ (see problem 8) $\sin 23° = \frac{BC}{AB}$ $0.391 = \frac{386}{AB}$ $0.391 \times AB = 386$ $AB = \frac{386}{0.391} \approx 987$ m Using 350 m: $0.391 \times AB = 350$ $AB = \frac{350}{0.391} \approx 895$ m	**3** (Award 1 point for a correct answer, 2 points for correct student work.) If students do not have a correct measurement for $\angle A$ in problem 8, they should receive full credit if they used the angle they found correctly for this problem.	II/III
Total score points	**28**	

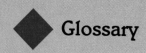

Glossary

The Glossary defines all vocabulary words indicated in this unit. It includes the mathematical terms that may be new to students, as well as words having to do with the contexts introduced in the unit. (Note: The Student Book has no Glossary. Instead, students are encouraged to construct their own definitions, based on their personal experiences with the unit activities.)

The definitions below are specific for the use of the terms in this unit. The page numbers given are from the Student Book.

alpha (α) (p. 28) the first letter of the Greek alphabet, used to represent an angle

beta (β) (p. 28) the second letter of the Greek alphabet, used to represent an angle

blind area (p. 10) an area that cannot be seen because something is blocking the view; a blind spot

blind spot (p. 10) an area that cannot be seen because something is blocking the view; a blind area

cosine of an angle (p. 51) in a right triangle, the ratio of the side adjacent to the angle to the hypotenuse

gamma (γ) (p. 28) the third letter of the Greek alphabet, used to represent an angle

glide angle (p. 36) the angle a glider makes with the ground as it descends

glide ratio (p. 34) the ratio of how far a glider will drop in height (h) to the distance (d) it travels in a horizontal direction, or h:d

sine ratio (p. 51) in a right triangle, the ratio of the side opposite the angle to the hypotenuse

steepness (p. 26) the ratio of the height (h) to the distance (d), or h:d

tangent of an angle (p. 37) in a right triangle, the ratio of the side opposite the angle to the side adjacent to the angle, or height:distance

vision line (p. 6) an imaginary straight line from a person's eye to an object

BRITANNICA
Mathematics
in
Context

Blackline
Masters

◆ Letter to the Family

Dear Family,

Your child will soon begin the *Mathematics in Context* unit *Looking at an Angle.* Below is a letter to your child that describes the unit and its goals.

In one section of the unit, your child will study how the angle of the sun or the distance of a light source affects the length of a shadow. You and your child might examine the changes in the length of a shadow of a tree and the corresponding angle of the sun at different times of the day. Your child then can model what you observed outside by holding a flashlight at different angles to change the length of the shadow of a household object.

You and your child might also talk about the blind spots that exist for the driver of a car. While you move to different positions around your parked car, your child can sit in the driver's seat and indicate when he or she cannot see you. Your child then can sketch diagrams of the car's blind spots.

We hope you enjoy these ways of "looking at an angle" with your child.

Sincerely,

The Mathematics in Context Development Team

Dear Student,

Welcome to *Looking at an Angle!*

In this unit, you will learn about vision lines and blind areas. Have you ever been on one of the top floors of a tall office or apartment building? When you looked out the window, were you able to see the sidewalk directly below the building? If you could see the sidewalk, it was in your field of vision; if you could not see the sidewalk, it was in a blind spot.

The relationship between vision lines and rays of light and the relationship between blind spots and shadows are some of the topics that you will explore in this unit. Have you ever noticed how the length of a shadow varies according to the time of day? As part of an activity, you will measure the length of the shadow of a stick and the corresponding angle of the sun at different times of the day. You will then determine how the angle of the sun affects the length of a shadow.

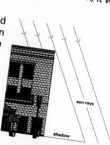

Besides looking at the angle of the sun, you will also study the angle that a ladder makes with the floor when it is leaning against a wall and the angle that a descending hang glider makes with the ground. You will learn two different ways to identify the steepness of an object: the angle the object makes with the ground and the tangent of that angle.

We hope you enjoy discovering the many ways of "looking at an angle."

Sincerely,

The Mathematics in Context Development Team

Name _____

Student Activity Sheet 1 ◆
Use with *Looking at an Angle*, page 7.

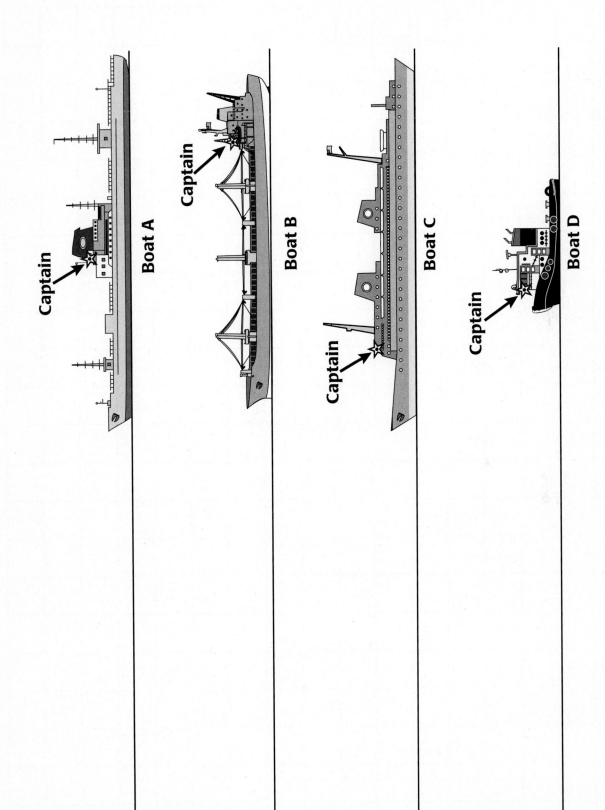

Captain
Boat A

Captain
Boat B

Captain
Boat C

Captain
Boat D

Student Activity Sheet 2

Use with *Looking at an Angle*,
pages 8 and 56.

Name _____

Student Activity Sheet 2

Name _____

Student Activity Sheet 3 ◆
Use with *Looking at an Angle*, page 11.

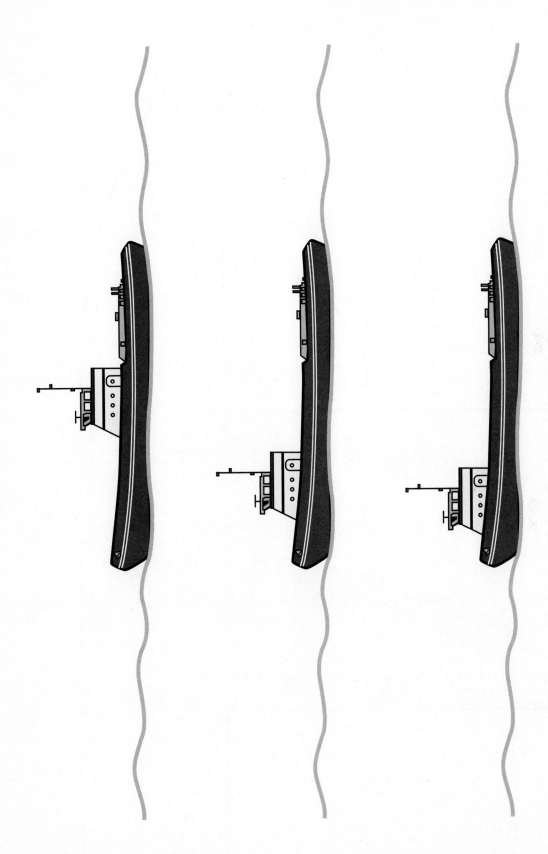

◆ **Student Activity Sheet 4**
Use with *Looking at an Angle*, page 16.

Name _____

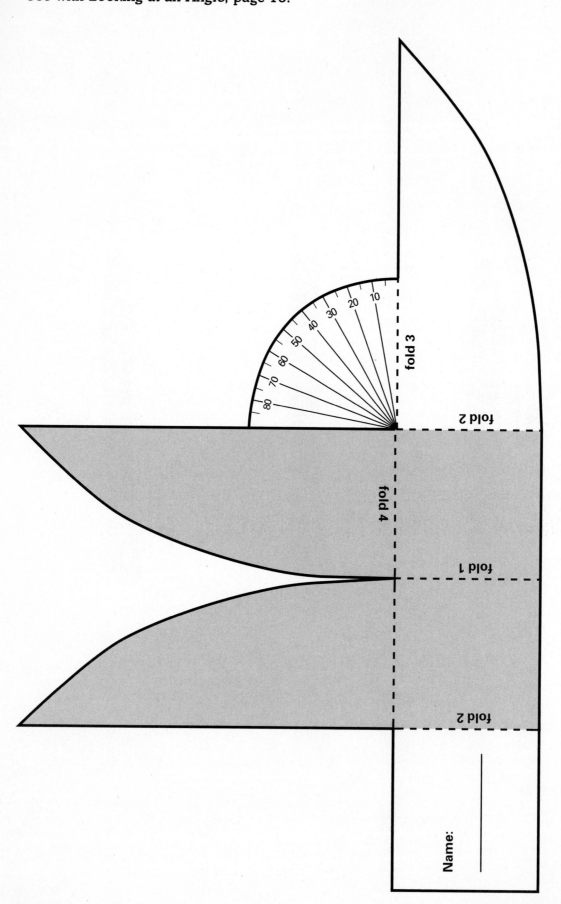

fold 3

fold 2

fold 4

fold 1

fold 2

Name:
_____

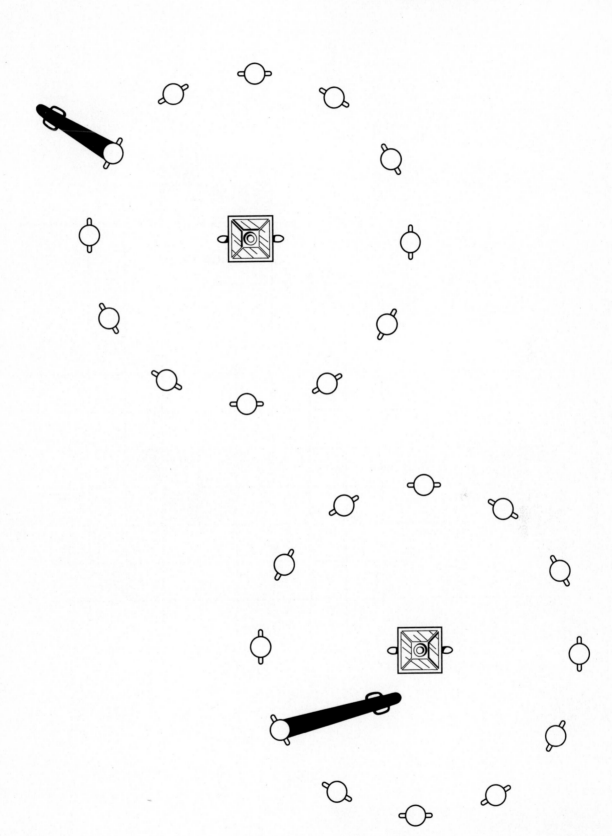

◆ **Student Activity Sheet 6**
Use with *Looking at an Angle*, page 21.

Name _____

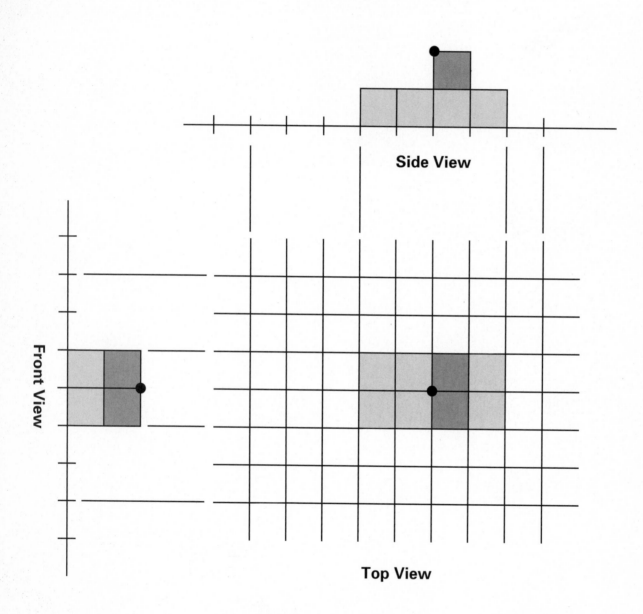

Side View

Front View

Top View

Name _____

Student Activity Sheet 7 ◆
Use with *Looking at an Angle*, page 21.

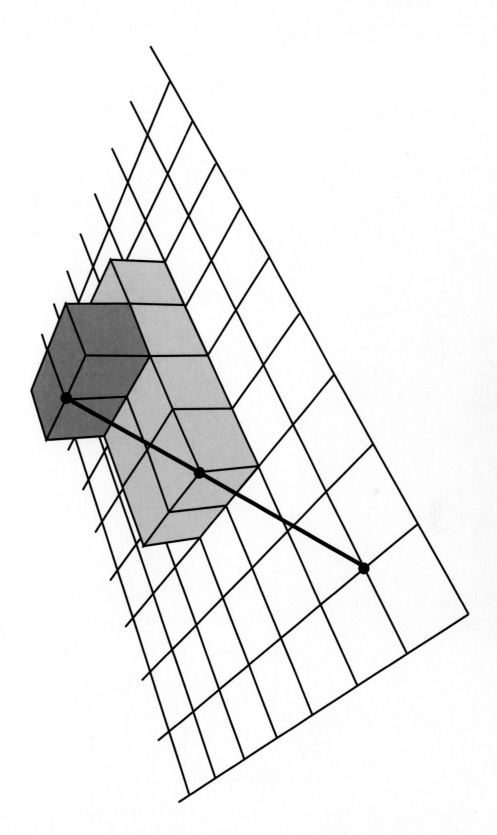

◆ **Student Activity Sheet 8**
Use with *Looking at an Angle*,
pages 22 and 23.

Name _____

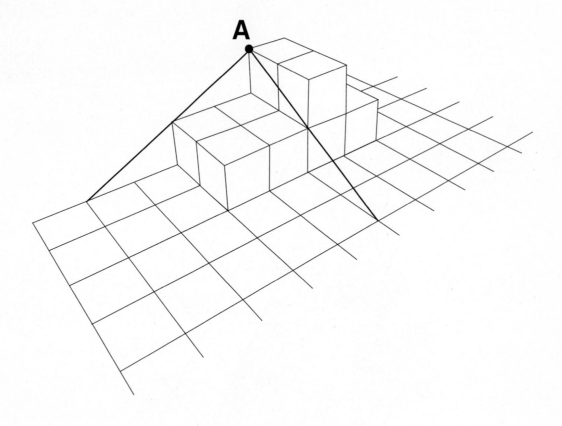

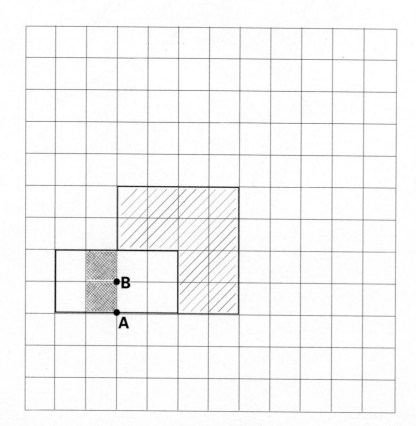

Name _____

Student Activity Sheet 9
Use with *Looking at an Angle*, page 24.

Picture A

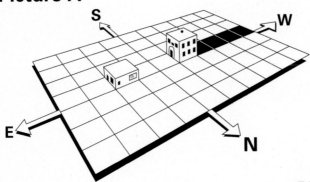

Picture B

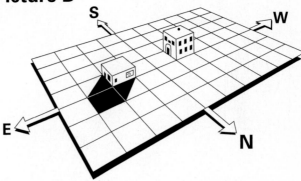

Picture C

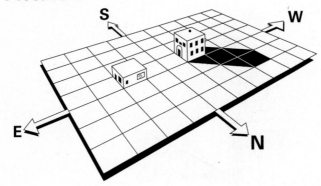

Picture D

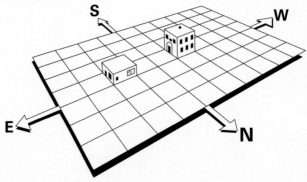

Student Activity Sheet 10
Use with *Looking at an Angle*, page 26.

Name _____

Picture A

Picture B

Name _____

Student Activity Sheet 11
Use with *Looking at an Angle*, page 43.

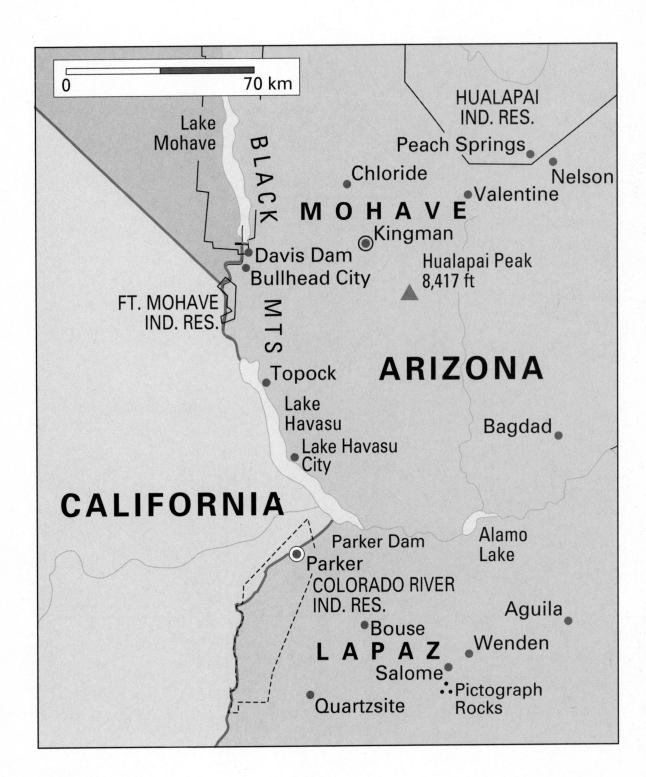

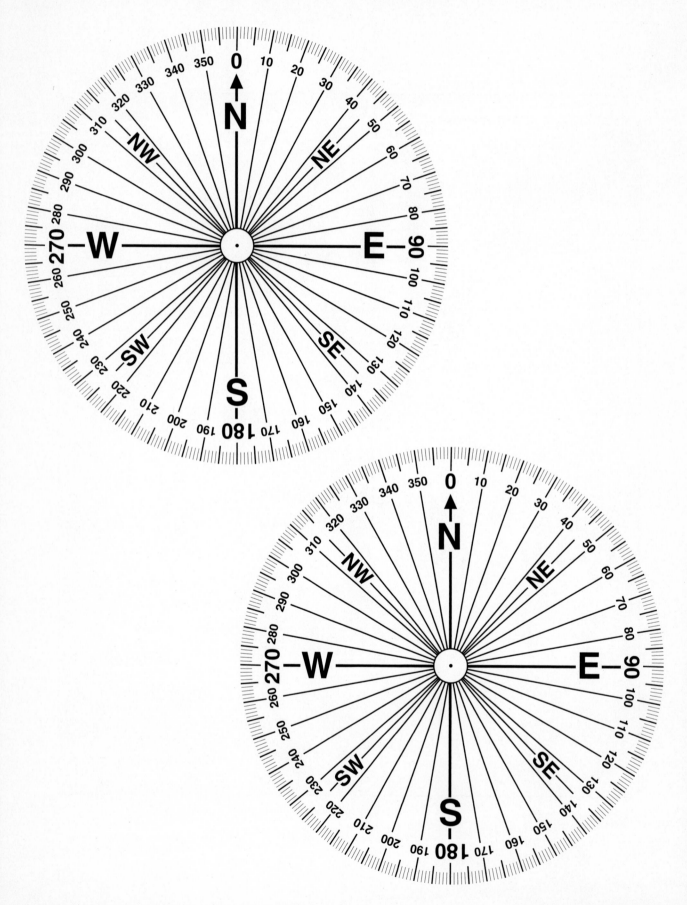